Quick and Cozy Recipes

Fast and Flavorful Creations

By

Teresa E. Musso

VEGETABLES.

*Preliminary Remarks—Potatoes—Boiled—Roasted—Baked—Fried—
Potato Balls—Ragoût—Purée—Omelette—To Brown—Potato Flour—
Jelly—Wall—To keep—Sweet Potatoes—Turnips—To Boil—Mash, &c.
—Beets—To Boil—Bake—Stew, &c.—Carrots—To Boil—Parsnips—
Oyster Plant—Green Peas—French Beans—Windsor Beans—String
Beans, &c.—To dress Egg Plant—Squashes—Rice—Green Corn—
Succatash—Hominy—Cabbage—Cauliflowers—Spinach—Celery—
Onions—Leeks—Artichokes—Tomatoes—Asparagus—Mushrooms.*

To dress Vegetables.—Vegetables should be fresh gathered, and washed quite clean; when not recently gathered, they should be put into cold spring-water sometime before they are dressed. When fresh gathered, they will not require so much boiling, by a third of the time, as when they have been gathered the usual time those in our markets have.

Shake the vegetables carefully to get out the insects; and take off the outside leaves.

To restore frost-bitten vegetables, lay them in cold water an hour before boiling, and put a piece of saltpetre in the saucepan when set on the fire.

Soft water is best for boiling vegetables; but if only hard water can be obtained, a very small bit of soda, or carbonate of ammonia, will soften it, and improve the appearance of the vegetables. Pearlash should never be used, as it imparts an unpleasant flavor, as will also soda if not cautiously used.

All vegetables (except carrots) should be boiled by themselves, and in plenty of water. Salt should be used with green vegetables; and the water should be skimmed before they are put in. Fast boiling, in an uncovered sauce-pan, will preserve their color. When they sink they are done, and should be taken out and drained, else they will lose their color, crispness, and flavor.

Green vegetables, generally, will require from twenty minutes to half an hour, fast boiling; but their age, freshness, and the season in which they are grown, require some variation of time. They should, almost invariably, be put on in boiling water.

Vegetables are very nutritious and wholesome, when thoroughly boiled; but are very indigestible when not sufficiently dressed. The principal points in cooking them are, to boil them so soft as to be easy of digestion, and sufficiently to get rid of any rankness, without losing their grateful flavor.

POTATOES.

Potatoes require no attention for the preservation of their color, but their *flavor* will be spoiled if their dressing be not attended to, which, although of the most simple nature, is frequently ill performed. The best mode of doing it is to sort the potatoes, and choose them of an equal size; wash them with a scrubbing-brush, and put them into cold water sufficient to cover them and no more. About ten minutes after the water has come to a boil, take out the half of it, and replace with cold water, to check it; the reason assigned for which is, "that the cold water sends the heat from the surface to the heart, and makes the potatoes mealy." Then throw in a large handful of salt, leave the pot uncovered, and let it remain upon the fire to simmer until the potatoes are done; this is the moment to be watched, for, if overboiled, they will become waxy. The cook should, therefore, occasionally try them, by piercing them to the heart with a fork, and, when they are tender, the pot should be instantly taken off the fire, and the potatoes passed through a cullender to drain; which being done, and the water thrown out, they should then be replaced upon a folded flannel, in the same pot, which should be left by the side of the fire to keep hot and to cause the evaporation of the steam. When served they should be wrapped in a warmed cotton napkin. If of moderate size they will take about half an hour boiling, to which 15 minutes must be added for evaporation ere they can be sent to table. An iron pot is the best vessel for boiling potatoes in, since, after the water has been poured off, it retains sufficient heat to dry them thoroughly.

Iron Pot, with Potato Strainer.

A good and economical mode of dressing potatoes, when soup, meat, or other eatables are to be boiled, is to have a tin strainer fitted to the mouth of the sauce-pan, so as to allow the steam to ascend from the boiler. By which simple contrivance *a* will boil the soup; *b*, when fixed in the pot, will steam the potatoes; and *c*, being the lid, will cover the whole, having a couple of small holes left in it to allow the steam to escape, in order to prevent it from falling down upon the potatoes.

Another way to Boil Potatoes.—Pare, wash, and throw them into a pan of cold water; then put them on to boil in a clean pot, with cold water sufficient to cover them, and sprinkle over a little salt; let them boil slowly *uncovered* till you can pass a fork through them; pour off the water, and set them where they will keep hot till wanted. When done in this way they are very mealy and dry.

Potatoes, either boiled or roasted, should *never be covered to* keep them hot.

To Boil New Potatoes.—These are never good unless freshly dug. Take them of equal size, and rub off the skins with a brush, or a very coarse cloth, wash them clean, and put them, without salt, into boiling, or at least, quite hot water; boil softly, and when they are tender enough to serve, pour off the water entirely, strew some fine salt over the potatoes, give them a shake, and let them stand by the fire in the sauce-pan for a minute, then dish and serve them immediately. Some cooks throw in a small slice of fresh butter, with the salt, and toss them gently in it after it is dissolved. This is a good mode, but the more usual one is to send melted butter to table with them, or to pour white sauce over them when they are very young, and served early in the season, as a side or corner dish.

Very small, 10 to 15 minutes moderate sized, 15 to 20 minutes.

New Potatoes in Butter.—Rub off the skins, wash the potatoes well, and wipe them dry; put them with three ounces of good butter, for a small dish, and with four ounces, or more, for a large one, into a well-tinned stew-pan or sauce-pan, and simmer them over a gentle fire for about half an hour. Keep them well shaken or tossed, that they may be equally done, and throw in some salt when they begin to stew. This is a good mode of dressing them when they are very young and watery.

To Boil Potatoes; (Captain Kater's Receipt.)—Wash, wipe, and pare the potatoes, cover them with cold water, and boil them gently until they are done; pour off the water, and sprinkle a little fine salt over them; then take each potato separately with a spoon, and lay it into a clean *warm* cloth, twist this so as to press all the moisture from the vegetable, and render it quite round; turn it carefully into a dish placed before the fire, throw a cloth over, and when all are done, send them to table quickly. Potatoes dressed in this way are mashed without the slightest trouble; it is also by far the best method of preparing them for puddings or for cakes.

To Roast or Bake Potatoes.—Scrub, and wash exceedingly clean, some potatoes nearly assorted in size; wipe them very dry, and roast them in a Dutch oven before the fire, placing them at a distance from it, and keeping them often turned; or, arrange them in a coarse dish, and bake them in a moderate oven. Dish them neatly in a napkin, and send them very hot to table; serve cold butter with them.

One and three-quarters to upwards of two hours.

Another way to Roast Potatoes.—Part oil, rub off the skin, and put them into the Dutch-oven, or, if there are embers, wrap them in two or three papers; wet the last, and cover them with the hot ashes, or bake them in the oven. Best of all, if the ashes are reduced and hot, to wash the potatoes clean, and bury them in them, which frees them from all moisture.

Scooped Potatoes (entremets); or second course dish.— Wash and wipe some large potatoes of a firm kind, and with a small scoop adapted to the purpose, form as many diminutive ones as will fill a dish; cover them with cold water, and when they have boiled gently for five minutes, pour it off, and put more cold water to them; after they have simmered a second time, for five minutes, drain the water quite away, and let them steam by the side of the fire from four to five minutes longer. Dish them carefully, pour white sauce over them, and serve them with the second course. Old potatoes thus prepared, have often been made to pass for *new* ones, at the best tables, at the season in which the fresh vegetable is dearest. The time required to boil them will of course vary with their quality: we give the method which we have found very successful.

Fried Potatoes (entremets).—After having washed them, wipe and pare some raw potatoes, cut them in slices of equal thickness, or into thin shavings, and throw them into plenty of boiling butter, or very pure clarified dripping. Fry them of a fine light brown, and very crisp; lift them out with a skimmer, drain them on a soft warm cloth, dish them very hot, and springle fine salt over them. This is an admirable way of dressing potatoes. When pared round and round to a corkscrew form, in ribbons or shavings of equal width, and served dry and well-fried, lightly piled in a dish, they make a hand-some appearance and are excellent eating. We have known them served with a slight sprinkling of Cayenne. If sliced, they should be something less than a quarter-inch thick.

Cold Potatoes.—They may be cut in slices somewhat less than half an inch thick, and fried in like manner. They are sometimes fried with onions as an accompaniment to pork chops, or a rasher of bacon.

Mashed Potatoes.—Boil them perfectly tender quite through, pour off the water, and steam them very dry; peel them quickly, take out every speck, and while they are still hot, press the potatoes through an earthen cullender, or bruise them to a smooth mash, with a strong wooden fork or spoon, but never pound them in a mortar, as that will reduce them to a close heavy paste. *Let them be entirely free from lumps,* for nothing can be more indicative of carelessness or want of skill on the part of the cook, than mashed potatoes sent to the table full of lumps. Melt in a clean sauce-pan a slice of good butter with a low spoonsful of milk, or, better still, of cream; put in the potatoes after having sprinkled some fine salt upon them, and stir the whole over a gentle fire, with a *wooden* spoon, until the ingredients are well mixed, and the whole is very hot. It may then be served directly; or heaped high in a dish, left rough on the surface, and browned before the fire; or it may be pressed into a well-buttered mould of handsome form, which has been strewed with the finest bread-crumbs, and shaken free of the loose ones, then turned out, and browned in an oven.

Obs.—More or less liquid will be required for potatoes of different kinds. For 2 pounds of potatoes add 1 tea-spoonful of salt, 1 ounce of butter and one-quarter pint of milk or sweet cream.

Potatoes a-la Maitre D'Hotel.—Cold potatoes that have been boiled should be used for this purpose. Lay them in a frying-pan with sufficient milk (or cream) to cover them, add a little butter, salt, and chopped parsley, and fry them until the milk thickens. They will be sufficiently cooked in a quarter of an hour, and make an excellent dish for breakfast.

Purée of Potatoes.—Mash the potatoes, and mix them while quite hot with some fine white gravy drawn from veal, together with butter and cream. The purée should be rather thin, and seasoned with salt, a very little pepper, and an atom of nutmeg.

Potato Omelette,—It may be made with a mashed potato or 2 ounces of potato-flour and 4 eggs, and seasoned with pepper, salt, and a little nutmeg. It should be made thick, and, being rather substantial; a squeeze of lemon will improve it. Fry a light brown.

Potato Balls.—Make mashed potatoes into balls with egg yolk, flour them, fry them in dripping, and drain them; or brown before the fire.

Ragoût of Potatoes.—Fry potato-balls, as above, drain them dry, and serve them covered with brown sauce.

To Brown Potatoes.—While the meat is roasting, and an hour before it is served, boil the potatoes and take off the skins; flour them well, and put them under the meat, taking care to dry them before they are sent to table. The kidney potatoes are best dressed in this way. The flouring is very essential.

Boiled Potatoes.—If waxy, or to be eaten with cold meat, they should be peeled and put whole upon the gridiron until nicely browned.

Potato Flour.—Rasp the potatoes into a tub of cold water, and change it repeatedly until the raspings fall to the bottom like paste; then dry it in the air, pound it in a mortar and pass it through a hair sieve. It is nearly as nutritive, and much lighter, than wheaten flour; it is, therefore, preferable for making puddings and pastry for infants and invalids; a portion of it also improves the appearance of household bread, and dealers constantly pass it off as arrowroot. If kept dry, it will remain good for years.

Potato Jelly.—Is made from the flour, only boiling water must be poured upon it, but care must be taken that it be absolutely boiling, or the complete change into jelly will not take place. It does not take many minutes to thus change a raw potato into this substance, which is not only highly nutritive, but extremely agreeable to the palate when flavored with a little sugar, nutmeg, and white wine.

Potato-Wall, or edging, to serve round fricassees, forms also a pretty addition to a corner dish.—Mash in a mortar as many boiled potatoes as you may want, with a good piece of butter; then, with the bowls of two silver spoons, raise a wall of it 2½ inches high within the rim of the dish to be used. Let the upper part be a little thinner than the lower; smooth it; and, after brushing it all over with egg, put it into the oven to become hot and a little colored. Before egging it, the outside may be ornamented with bits of paste cut into shapes,

---

To Keep Potatoes.—Buy them as dug from the ground, without taking off the earth that adheres to them, and *never wash them till they are wanted to be dressed.* Place them in a dry cellar, upon straw, and cover them in winter with straw or mats, to guard them from the frost.

Obs.—Potatoes should always be *boiled* a little before being put into stews, &c, as the first water in which they are boiled is of a poisonous quality.

Sweet Potatoes.—These are better roasted or baked, than boiled.

To bake them, wash them clean and wipe them dry; then place them in a quick oven. They will take from half an hour to an hour, according to their size.

To roast them; prepare them as for baking, and either cook them in the hot ashes of a wood fire, or in a Dutch oven. They will take from half to three-quarters of an hour.

To boil them; wash them carefully, put them in a pot with just water enough to cover them; let them boil from one-half to three-quarters of an hour; try them with a fork to see if they are done.

TURNIPS.

To boil Turnips.—Pare entirely from them the stringy rind, and either split the turnips once or leave them whole; throw them into boiling water slightly salted, and keep them closely covered from smoke and dust till they are tender. When small and young they will be done in from 15 to 20 minutes; at their full growth they will require from three-quarters to a full hour, or more, of gentle boiling. After they become old and woolly, they are not worth dressing in any way. When boiled in their skins and pared afterwards, they are said to be of better flavor and much less watery than when cooked in the usual way.

Young turnips, 15 to 20 minutes: full grown, three quarters to one hour, or more.

To mash Turnips.—Split them once or even twice should they be large; after they are pared, boil them very tender, and press the water thoroughly from them with a couple of trenchers, or with the back of a large plate and one trencher. To ensure their being free from lumps, it is better to pass them through a cullender or coarse hair-sieve, with a wooden spoon; though, when quite young, they may be worked sufficiently smooth without this. Put them into a clean sauce-pan, and stir them constantly for some minutes over a gentle fire, that they may be very dry; then add some salt, a bit of fresh butter, and a little cream, or in lieu of this new milk (we would also recommend a seasoning of white pepper or Cayenne, when appearance and fashion are not particularly regarded), and continue to simmer and to stir them for five or six minutes longer, or until they have quite absorbed all the liquid which has been poured to them. Serve them always as hot as possible. This is an excellent receipt.

Turnips, weighed after they are pared, 3 lbs.: dried 5 to 8 minutes. Salt, 1 tea-spoonful; butter, 1 oz. to 1½ oz.; cream or milk, nearly half pint: 5 or 6 minutes.

Turnips in White Sauce. (Entremets.)—When no scoop for the purpose is at hand, cut some small finely-grained turnips into quarters, and pare them into balls, or into the shape of plums or pears of equal size; arrange them evenly in a broad stew-pan or sauce-pan, and cover them nearly with good veal broth, throw in a little salt, and a morsel of sugar, and boil them rather quickly until they are quite tender, but unbroken; lift them out, draining them well from the broth; dish, and pour over them some thick white sauce. As an economy, a cup of cream, and a tea-spoonful of arrowroot may be added to the broth in which the turnips have stewed, to make the sauce; and when it boils, a small slice of butter may be stirred and well worked into it should it not be sufficiently rich without.

Turnips stewed in Butter. (Good.)—This is an excellent way of dressing the vegetable when it is mild and finely grained; but its flavor otherwise is too strong to be agreeable. After they have been washed, wiped quite dry, and pared, slice the turnips nearly half an inch thick, and divide them into dice. Just dissolve an ounce of butter for each half-pound of the turnips, put them in as flat as they can be, and stew them very gently indeed, from three-quarters of an hour to a full hour Add a seasoning of salt and white pepper when they are half done. When thus prepared, they may be dished over fried or nicely broiled mutton cutlets, or served by themselves.

For a small dish: turnips, 1½ lb.; butter, 3 oz.; seasoning of white pepper; salt, half tea-spoonful, or more: three-quarters to one hour. Large dish, turnips, 2 lbs.; butter, 4 ozs.

Turnips in Gravy.—To a pound of turnips sliced and cut into dice, pour a quarter-pint of boiling veal gravy, add a small lump of sugar, some salt and Cayenne, or white pepper, and boil them quickly 50 to 60 minutes. Serve them very hot.

Turnip-Tops.—Should be nicely picked, (as the full leaves are coarse and strong,) and thrown into cold water an hour before boiling; put them on in plenty of boiling water, with salt, and they will be done in about 20 minutes; when press them dry.

BEETS.

To boil Beets.—Wash the roots delicately clean, but neither scrape nor cut them, as not a fibre even should be trimmed away, until after they are dressed. Throw them into boiling water, and according to their size boil them from one hour and a half to two hours and a half. Pare and serve them whole, or thickly sliced, and send melted butter to table with them. Beet-root is often mixed with winter salads; and it makes a pickle of beautiful color; but one of the most usual modes of serving it at the present day is, with the cheese, cold and mere by pared and sliced, after having been boiled or baked.

Boiled, 1½ to 2½ hours; baked, 2½ to 3½ hours.

Obs.—This root must not be probed with a fork like other vegetables, to ascertain if it be done or not; but the cook must endeavor, by attention, to learn the time required for it. After it is lifted out, the thickest part may be pressed with the fingers, to which it will yield, if it be sufficiently boiled.

To bake Beets.—Beet-root, if slowly and carefully baked until it is tender quite through, is very rich and sweet in flavor, although less bright in color than when it is boiled: it is also, we believe, remarkably nutritious and wholesome. Wash and wipe it very dry, but neither cut nor break any part of it: then lay it into a coarse dish, and bake it in a gentle oven for 4 or 5 hours: it will sometimes require even a longer time than this. Pare it quickly, if to be served hot; but leave it to cool first, when it is to be sent to table cold.

The white beet-root is dressed exactly like the red: the leaves of it are boiled and served like asparagus.

Bake in slow oven from 4 to 6 hours.

Stewed Beet.—Bake or boil it tolerably tender, and let it remain until it is cold, then pare and cut it into slices; heat and stew it for a short time in some good pale veal gravy (or in strong veal broth for ordinary occasions), thicken this with a tea-spoonful of arrow-root, and half a cupful or more of good cream, and stir in, as it is taken from the fire, from a tea-spoon to a table-spoonful of vinegar. The beet may be served likewise in thick white sauce, to which, just before it is dished, mild eschalots may be added.

CARROTS.

To boil Carrots.—Wash the mould from them, and scrape the skin off lightly with the edge of a sharp knife, or, should this be objected to, pare them as thin and as equally as possible; in either case free them from all blemishes, and should they be very large, split them across the tops a few inches down; rinse them well, and throw them into plenty of boiling water with some salt in it. The skin of very young carrots may be rubbed off like that of new potatoes, and from 20 to 30 minutes will then be sufficient to boil them; but at their full growth they will require from 1½ to 2 hours. It was formerly the custom to tie them in a cloth, and to wipe the skin from them with it after they were dressed; and old-fashioned cooks still use one to remove it; but all vegetables should be served with the least possible delay. Melted butter should accompany boiled carrots.

PARSNEPS.

To boil Parsneps.—Parsnips are cooked as carrots, but they do not require so much boiling, and are sometimes served differently, being mashed with some butter, a little cream or milk, and seasoned with pepper and salt.

Parsneps are also excellent fried.

Parsnep Fritters.—Boil 6 parsneps tender; then skin and mash them; mix with them 1 or 2 eggs well beaten, and 2 tea-spoonsful of wheat flour. Make them up in small cakes, and fry them in a little lard or beef gravy, made boiling hot before the cakes are put in. A little salt should be added to the lard or gravy.

SALSIFY, OR OYSTER PLANTS.

Salsify, or Oyster Plants.—Scrape the salsify, cut it in long strips, and parboil it, then chop it up fine with egg batter.

It is sometimes served with the roots whole, having been first thoroughly boiled and then fried in egg batter.

PEAS.

Green Peas.—Boil them very fast in plenty of water with the lid off the stew-pan; the water should be moderately salted. They are unfit for eating when they become hard and yellowish, but when growing rather old a very small quantity of carbonate of ammonia put into the water, with 2 or 3 lumps of loaf-sugar, will greatly improve them. The old English method of putting a sprig of mint, or a little parsley, is still a good practice, and ought to be continued unless specially forbidden, or the mint may be chopped and put round the dish. A few bits of raw butter should also be put into the peas when boiled, and a dust of pepper and salt thrown over them if they be completely ripe; but if quite young, neither butter, salt, nor pepper should be added to them, but a tea-spoonful of pounded white sugar. When growing to maturity the pods are of different ages, and young and old peas should not be boiled together; sift them, therefore, from each other, and put the old ones into the water some minutes sooner than the young: they require from 15 to 20 minutes boiling.

Another way to boil Green Peas.—Having shelled them, put a tea-spoonful of white sugar and some salt into the water, and when it boils, put in the peas, with a small bunch of mint; boil 20 minutes, or until they are done; then drain them in a cullender; put a piece of butter into the dish, with the peas, stir them about, and serve.

A peck of peas will require a gallon of water to boil them in.

To stew Green Peas.—Put into a stew-pan a quart of peas, one onion, two ounces of butter, a sprig of mint, a tea-spoonful of white sugar, and two table-spoonsful of gravy; stew till soft, when take out the onion and mint, and thicken with flour and butter. A lettuce is sometimes stewed with them.

Peas dressed together should be as nearly one size as possible, else some only will be properly done. To ensure this the peas should be passed through a coarse sieve.

To stew Old Peas.—Soak a quart of good boiling peas in water an hour, and put them into a stew-pan, with weak gravy, a slice of lean bacon, and a tea-spoonful of white sugar; stew till tender, when take out the bacon, and mix well with the peas a beaten egg or two, and a bit of butter rolled in flour.

Split-Peas Pudding.—Take any quantity, say 1 pint of yellow split peas; allow them to remain in water the whole night before you wish to use them; after which take them out and put them into a cloth so loose as to allow the peas to swell; boil them for 4 hours, or until they are quite tender, then rub them through a cullender, so as to render them perfectly smooth; add to the pulp a lump of butter and some salt. After being well mixed put the peas again into a cloth, tie tightly, and boil for about half an hour. Pour over it melted butter.

A richer pudding may be made if two well-beaten eggs are added along with the butter. It is served with boiled pork.

To preserve Peas for Winter use.—Gather them when ripe, for if too young they will be watery Shell them, put then in strong jars, or open-mouthed bottles, and shake them to make them sit closely together. Cork the jars tightly; place them in any iron pot large enough to contain them, with hay between them to prevent breakage; fill the pot with cold water up to the neck of the jars, and allow it to boil 1½ hour if in cool moist weather, but for 2 hours if it be hot and dry. Do not take the jars out of the pot till the water is cold.

Obs.—French beans and asparagus may be preserved in the same manner; they retain their color, but lose much of their flavor, and require a little sugar to improve it.

BEANS.

To boil Windsor Beans.—When young, freshly gathered, and well dressed, these beans, even with many persons accustomed to a luxurious table, are a favorite accompaniment to a dish of streaked bacon, or delicate pickled pork. Shell them only just before they are wanted, then wash, drain, and throw them into boiling water, salted as for peas. When they are quite tender, pour them into a hot cullender, drain them thoroughly, and send them to table quickly, with a tureen of parsley and butter, or with plain melted butter, when it is preferred. A boiled cheek of bacon, trimmed free of any blackened parts, may be dished *over* the beans, upon occasion.

From 20 to 30 minutes; less when *very* young.

Obs.—When the skin of the beans appear wrinkled, they will generally be found sufficiently tender to serve, but they should be tasted to ascertain that they are so.

To stew.—Take them when too old to dress any other way, boil them, and remove the tough outer skin by peeling it off after the beans are boiled; thicken some white broth with a little cream or flour and butter, add the beans to it, and stew them all together over the fire for a few minutes. Add pepper and salt to palate.

To boil French, or String Beans.—When early and young, they should be clipped and cut finely, or almost shred, and thrown into cold water; then put them on in boiling water with some salt, and boil till tender.

When the beans are older, cut off the ends, strip off the strings, and cut each bean into 4 or 8 pieces; and boil as above.

To preserve the fine green color of beans, cover them as soon as done with melted butter.

String Beans fricasseed.—When nearly boiled tender, strain the beans, and put them into a stew-pan with a tea-cupful of white gravy; add 2 table-spoonsful of cream, a little butter and flour, simmer a few minutes, season, and serve.

String Beans a la Français (an excellent Receipt).—Prepare as many young and freshly gathered beans as will serve for a large dish, boil them tender, and drain the water well from them. Melt a couple of ounces of fresh butter, in a clean sauce-pan and stir smoothly to it a small dessert-spoonful of flour; keep these well shaken and gently simmered until they are lightly browned, add salt and pepper, and pour to them by degrees a small cupful of good veal gravy, (or, in lieu of this, of sweet rich cream,) toss the beans in the sauce until they are as hot as possible; stir quickly in, as they are taken from the fire, the beaten yolks of 2 fresh eggs, and a little lemon juice, and serve them without delay. The eggs and lemon are sometimes omitted, and a table-spoonful of minced parsley is added to the butter and flour; but this, we think, is scarcely an improvement.

Beans, 1 to 2 quarts: boiled 15 to 20 minutes. Butter, 2 oz.; flour, 1 dessert-spoonful; salt and pepper; veal gravy, a *small* cupful; yolks of egg, 2; lemon juice, a dessert-spoonful.

To dress Dried French Beans.—Boil for more than 2 hours, in 2 quarts of water, a pound of the seeds or beans of scarlet runners; fill a pint basin with onions peeled or sliced, brown them in a sauce-pen, with rather more than a quarter of a pound of fresh butter; stir them constantly; strain the water from the beans, and mix them with the onions; add a tea-spoonful of pepper, some salt, and a little gravy. Let them stew for 10 minutes, and stir in the beaten yolks of 2 eggs, and a table-spoonful of vinegar. Serve them hot.

To stew Red Beans.—Put 1 pint of red beans in 2 quarts of water, and let them soak over night. Drain off the water early the next morning and place them over the fire in 2 quarts of fresh water. When they are perfectly soft break them a little without throwing off the water; add 2 table-spoonsful of butter; season with pepper, salt, parsley, thyme, and add an onion. When the beans are soft and mashed, let them simmer slowly till dinner.

Lima Beans.—Wash in cold water 1 quart of Lima beans shelled; then put them in a stew-pan with just enough boiling water to cover them. Let them boil, with the stew-pan closely covered for half an hour; then try them to see if they are tender; turn off almost all the water, and add a tea-cup nearly full of butter, salt and pepper to your taste. Stir them well together. Heat them for a few minutes longer and serve.

EGG-PLANT.

To dress Egg-Plant.—Parboil the egg-plants till they become soft, then cut them in half lengthwise. Scoop out the inside, leaving the skin whole; take half of a small onion to about seven egg-plants, with half pound of butter, and put them over the fire in a pot for a few moments; then mix with it half a good-sized loaf of bread which has been soaked in milk; mix it all well together; put in salt, black and red pepper, and a little parsley, and let it stew an hour. Then take some grated toast and strew over it, and put it for half an hour over the coals on a gridiron, then return the mixture to the shells, and serve them.

A very fine way to dress. Egg-Plant.—Take as many eggplants as the size of your family requires—pare, quarter and boil them till soft enough to mash like turnips. Mash them, add a little bread crumb soaked in milk, butter, chopped parsley, an onion boiled and mashed, some butter, pepper, and salt. Mix these well together, and pour it into a baking dish; cover the top with grated bread, and bake it for half an hour.

Another way to dress Egg Plant.—Split the egg-plant in half-parboil it until soft enough to scrape out the inside, leaving the shell whole. Take an onion cut up, pepper, salt, parsley, and one egg. Sprinkle in a little flour; stew all together with a lump of butter, in a sauce-pan, until thoroughly cooked. Then put them in the shells, sprinkle them with crumbs of bread, and bake them till brown.

To fry Egg-Plant.—Cut the egg-plant into slices quarter of an inch thick; let it lie for several hours in salted water to remove the bitter taste. Heat a small quantity of butter; when very hot, put in the slices; turn them when one side is done. Let them cook thoroughly.

Summer Squashes or Cymbelins.—When these vegetables are fresh, the rind will be crisp when cut by the nail. If very young and tender, they may be boiled whole; if not, pare them. Extract the seeds and strings, cut them small, put them in a stew-pan with water enough just to cover them; add one tea-spoonful of salt to each common sized squash; boil them till the pieces break; half an hour is generally enough, and then press them through a culender with a skimmer. Mix them with butter to your taste, and a little salt if necessary.

Winter Squash.—This requires rather more boiling than the summer kind. Pare it, cut it in pieces, take out the seeds and strings; boil it in a very little water till it is quite soft. Then press out the water, mash it, and add butter, salt, and pepper to your taste.

From half to three-quarters of an hour will generally suffice to cook it.

RICE.

To Boil Rice.—Wash the rice perfectly clean, and put on one pound in two quarts of cold water; stir it up from the bottom of the kettle once or twice, till it boils; let it boil twenty minutes, strain it through a sieve, and put it before the fire; shake, it up with a fork every now and then, to separate the grains, and make it quite dry. Serve it hot.

To Boil Rice Carolina Fashion.—Wash and pick the rice in cold water, which, when you are ready for the rice, pour off. Put it in a pot of boiling water, already salted. Boil it hard for 20 minutes; then take it off the fire, and pour off the water Set the pot in the chimney corner with the lid off, while dishing the dinner, to allow the rice to dry. Each grain will then be separate and free from moisture.

Casserole de Riz aux Œufs.—Clean and wash 6 ounces of rice, put it into a stew-pan with cold water, and, after it has boiled for about a minute, strain it; then add twice the quantity of broth, and let it stew gently until the rice will break easily with a spoon. Should the liquor dry too much before the rice is soft enough, add a little more broth. Work it well with stock and an egg beaten, as the rice should be firm and well blended; then make it into a wall, lining the inside of a mould of the requisite height; bake the casserole. Take the white portion of cold fowl, cold veal, or sweetbreads; mince them finely, add some thick white sauce and mushrooms, fill the casserole, and cover the top with poached eggs; cover them with glaze, and serve it up very hot.

GREEN CORN.

Sweet or sugar corn is best for boiling. Trim off the husks, excepting the inside leaves; throw the corn into boiling water with a little salt in it, and let it boil from one-half to three-quarters of an hour, according to its size. Then take off the remaining husks, and serve the corn, laid in a dish on a napkin;

let the corners of the napkin be thrown over the corn, to keep it hot. It is eaten with salt and butter.

Or:—Cut the corn from the cob and put it in a stew-pan, with a tea-cupful of water to each quart of corn; cover it closely, and let it stew gently for nearly one hour; then add half a tea-cupful of butter, and pepper and salt to your taste.

Common white corn may be improved by the addition of a little white sugar. To roast it, take off the husks, and lay it over the coals on a gridiron, turning it occasionally.

Succatash.—Take 12 ears of sweet corn, and cut the kernels from the cob; string 1 quart of green beans, and cut them in small pieces; wash them, and put them with the corn in a stew-pan with half a pint of boiling water; milk may be used if preferred. Let them boil three-quarters of an hour, closely covered; then add a piece of butter the size of a large egg a tea-spoonful of salt, and a little pepper; stir them well together; cover them for ten minutes, and serve them.

Half a pound of salt fat pork cut in slices may be substituted for the butter.

Lima beans and corn make a still finer succatash than string beans.

Corn Pudding—to be eaten as a vegetable.—Grate ears of green corn; add to a quart of it a tea-cupful of cream or milk, a lump of butter about the size of an egg, and a tea-spoonful of salt. Mix all well together; put it in your dish and bake it an hour and a half. To be eaten as a vegetable, with butter, pepper and salt.

Hominy.—There are three sizes of hominy. Large hominy requires to be boiled from 4 to 5 hours over a gentle fire. It should be washed clean, and put in the stew-pan with just enough water to cover it. It is eaten as a vegetable. To cook the smaller hominy, wash it in two waters; then, to one tea-cupful of hominy, add a quart of water and a tea-spoonful of salt, and place the dish that contains it in a kettle of boiling water, to prevent it from getting burnt, or else over a very gentle fire. Let it boil for an hour, stirring it well with a spoon. It is generally eaten for breakfast. It is excellent, sliced and fried, after it has become cold.

CABBAGES.

To boil Cabbage and Greens.—A full-grown cabbage, quartered, will require an hour's boiling; a young one, half that time. Greens will require about 20 minutes quick boiling. In both cases, salt should be put into the water.

Savoys should be boiled whole, and quartered before serving.

It has been recommended to boil cabbages in two waters; that is, when they are half done to pour off the water, and add fresh boiling water.

Be careful to press the greens as dry as possible.

Sauer Kraut.—Shred very finely 6 white cabbages, having cut out the stalks; mix with them half a pound of salt, and press them as closely as possible into a cask; put over a cloth, then a wooden, cover, and upon that a heavy weight: let it stand in a warm cellar 2 months, keeping the liquor that rises on it, and it will be fit for use: it should then be removed to a cooler, place. In Germany, half an ounce of juniper berries, anniseed, or caraway seeds, would be added to the above; but this is not recommended for American taste.

To dress Sauer Kraut.—Put a quart into a stew-pan with a little butter, and half a pint of weak gravy; stew gently until tender, and serve under boiled pork or beef, or sausages, boiled or fried. The Bavarian method of dressing sauer kraut is, after it has been boiled, to mix it with butter and red wine.

To stew Cabbage.—Parboil in milk and water, and drain it, then shred it, put it into a stew-pan, with a small piece of butter, a small tea-cupful of cream, and seasoning, and stew tender. Or, it may be stewed in white or brown gravy.

To stew Red Cabbage.—Shred finely half a cabbage, and put it into a stew-pan, with a tea-cupful of gravy, and 2 oz. of butter; stew slowly till tender, season with salt and serve. To heighten the color of the cabbage, a slice or two of beetroot may be added, but should be taken out before serving.

Another Way (Flemish Receipt).—Strip the outer leaves from a fine and fresh red cabbage; wash it well, and cut it into the thinnest possible slices, beginning at the top; put it into a thick sauce-pan in which two or three ounces of good butter have been just dissolved; add some pepper and salt, and stew it very slowly indeed for 3 or 4 hours in its own juice, keeping it often stirred, and well pressed down. When it is perfectly tender add a table-spoonful of vinegar; mix the whole up thoroughly, heap the cabbage in a hot dish, and serve broiled sausages round it; or omit these last, and substitute lemon juice, cayenne pepper, and half a cupful of good gravy.

The stalk of the cabbage should be split in quarters, and taken entirely out in the first instance.

To boil Cauliflowers.—Choose those that are close and white, cut off the green leaves, and look carefully that there are no caterpillars about the stalk; soak an hour in cold water, with a handful of salt in it; then boil them in milk and water, and take care to skim the sauce-pan, that not the least foulness may fall on the flower. It must be served very white, and rather crimp.

In White Sauce.—Take off the whole of the leaves of a cauliflower, and half boil it; then cut it into handsome pieces and lay them in a stew-pan with a little broth, a bit of mace, a little salt, and a dust of white pepper; simmer half an hour, but let the stalk be put down quarter of an hour before the flower; then put a little cream, butter, and flour; shake, and simmer a few minutes, and serve.

To boil Brocoli.—Peel the stalks, and boil them 15 minutes with a little salt in the water; tie the shoots into bunches, and boil half the above time; serve with melted butter or toast.

SPINACH.

Spinach, (Entremets,) French receipt.—Pick the spinach leaf by leaf from the stems, and wash it in abundance of spring water, changing it several times; then shake it in a dry cloth held by the four corners, or drain it on a large sieve. Throw it into sufficient well-salted boiling water to allow it to float freely, and keep it pressed down with a skimmer that it may be equally done. When quite young it will be tender in from eight to ten minutes, but to ascertain if it be so, take a leaf and squeeze it between the fingers. If to be dressed in the French mode, drain, and then throw it directly into plenty of fresh water, and when it is cool form it into balls and press the moisture thoroughly from it with the hands. Next, chop it extremely fine upon a clean trencher; put two ounces (for a large dish) of butter into a stew-pan or bright thick sauce-pan, lay the spinach on it, and keep it stirred over a gentle fire for ten minutes, or until it appears dry; dredge in a spoonful of flour, and turn the spinach as it is added; pour to it gradually a few spoonsful of very rich veal gravy, or, if preferred, of *good* boiling cream, (with the last of these a dessert-spoonful or more of pounded sugar maybe added for a second-course dish, when the true French mode of dressing the vegetable is liked.) Stew the whole briskly until the whole is well absorbed; dish, and serve the spinach very hot, with small, pale fried sippets round it, or with leaves of puff paste fresh from the oven, or well dried after having been fried. For ornament, the sippets may be fancifully shaped with a tin cutter.

A proper seasoning of salt must not be omitted in this or any other preparation of the spinach.

———

Spinach, (common English mode.)—Boil the spinach very green in plenty of water, drain, and then press the moisture from it between two trenchers; chop it small, put it into a clean sauce-pan, with a slice of fresh butter, and stir the whole until well mixed and very hot. Smooth it in a dish, mark it in dice, and send it quickly to table.

———

Eggs and Spinach.—Boil and mince the spinach, and serve upon it the eggs, poached; or, stew spinach, or sorrel, and place the poached eggs round the dish, with pieces of fried bread between them.

———

To stew Celery.—Wash the heads, and strip off their outer leaves; either halve or leave them whole, according to their size, and cut them into lengths of 4 inches. Put them into a stew-pan with a cup of broth or weak white gravy; stew till tender; then add 2 spoonsful of cream, a little flour and butter, seasoned with pepper, salt, nutmeg, and a little pounded white sugar; and simmer all together.

Or:—Parboil it, cut it into quarters, fry it, and serve it on a napkin, or with beef gravy.

Celery is a great improvement to all soups and gravies, and much used as a white sauce, either alone or with oysters.

———

CUCUMBERS.

To stew Cucumbers.—Pare eight or ten large cucumbers, and cut them into thick slices, flour them well, and fry them in butter; then put them into a sauce-pan with a tea-cupful of gravy; season it with Cayenne, salt and catsup. Let them stew for an hour, and serve them hot.

———

Boiled Cucumbers. Dr. Kitchiner's receipt.—Cucumbers may be cut into quarters and boiled like asparagus, and served up with toasted bread and melted butter. This is a most delicate way of preparing cucumbers for the dinner are, and they are a most luscious and savory dish.

ONIONS.

To Preserve Onions.—Onions should be pulled up as soon as their tops are nearly dead, or they will push out fresh roots after rain, which will greatly injure their bulbs, and prevent, their keeping sound.

Being gathered in September, they should be spread thin on the ground, in the full sun; turn them over once or twice daily, until they are thoroughly dried, and then store them in a well-aired loft; lay them thinly, string them up by the tails, or hang them in nets. The outer husks should be taken off before housing, as should also the tails, if the onions are not to be strung. String them thus:—tie three or four onions by the tails, with matting, or packthread; then place on two or three more onions and bind the thread once or twice round their tails; place and bind more onions, and so on. In this manner is made a string or rope of onions, which will keep, if hung up in a dry, well-aired place, free from frost. If onions begin to sprout, sear the roots with a hot iron, which will check the vegetation.

To Boil Onions Plain.—Peel them and soak them an hour in cold water; put them into boiling milk and water, boil them till tender, and serve with melted butter. Or, boil the onions in two waters.

To Stew Onions.—Peel them, flour, and fry them in a little butter, a light brown; then put them into weak gravy, season, and stew slowly two hours. Dish them up-side down, with the sauce over them. In peeling, be careful not to cut the top or bottom too closely, else the onion will not keep whole.

Baked or Roasted Onions. Put them, as taken from the store-room, into a tin, and bake in a moderate oven; or, roast in a Dutch oven. Serve with cold butter in a small plate. The outer peel should not be removed until the onions are to be eaten.

Ragoût of Onions.—Boil button onions, peeled, until they are tender; put them into brown sauce, and add salt.

Or: having peeled the onions, brown them in a Dutch oven, and put them into a stew-pan with any meat bones, a slice of lean bacon, a little water, and some pepper; stew them till tender, when take out the bone and bacon, and thicken the gravy.

The onions should be spread in one layer in the stew pan.

Leeks—Are generally looked upon as a species of onion, and, as such, commonly employed in the same manner, though rather milder in flavor. If boiled in separate waters, changing it 3 or 4 times, until stewed quite tender, then served in white sauce, or quartered and placed upon toast like asparagus, they will eat nearly, if not quite, as delicate.

ARTICHOKES.

Boiled.—Cut the stalk even, trim off a few of the outside leaves and the points of the others. If young, half an hour will boil them. Serve them with melted butter in as many small cups as there are artichokes, to help with each.

Or: Cut the artichokes in 4, remove the choke, trim the pieces neatly, boil them quickly in salt water, dish them, laying the leaves outwards, and pour melted butter or white sauce over the bottoms.

Stewed.—Strip off the leaves, remove the choke, and soak them in warm water for two or three hours, changing the water every hour; then put them into a stew-pan with a piece of butter rolled in Cayenne pepper and flour; a tea-cupful of gravy, and a spoonful or two of catsup or other sauce; add a spoonful of vinegar, or one of lemon-juice, before serving; let all stew till the artichokes are quite tender, and, if necessary, thicker the sauce with a little more butter.

Artichoke Bottoms.—If dried, must be soaked, then stewed in weak gravy, or baked and served with or without forcemeat in each. Or they may be boiled in milk, and served with cream-sauce or added to ragoûts, French pies, &c.

They may also be dipped in batter and fried, then served with a sauce made of fine herbs, a spoonful of oil, and the juice of lemon.

A-la Poivrade.—Take very small artichokes, cut them in quarters from the bottom, and remove the choke. Serve them in a little cold water, like radishes; make a sauce with oil, vinegar, pepper, and salt: they have the flavor of nuts.

Jerusalem Artichokes—Should be boiled, putting them at first into cold water, and must be taken up the moment they are done, or they will be too soft.

They may be boiled plain, or served with white fricassee-sauce. When boiled, if rubbed through a sieve with a little fresh butter and cream, they form an excellent purêe as a sauce for cutlets, or as a thickening for some sorts of white soup; or they may be sliced and fried.

TOMATOES.

To stew Tomatoes.—Take 10 large tomatoes—put them into a pan, and pour scalding water over them to remove the skins easily; peel them and cut out all the hard or unripe portion; then cut them through and take out the seeds. Boil an onion and mash it fine, add it to the tomatoes with pepper and salt to your taste, and a piece of butter as large as a hen's egg. Put them on to stew in an earthen pipkin, and let them simmer 2 hours. A quarter of an hour before dinner is ready, add 4 or 5 table-spoonsful of grated bread, and let it all stew till ready to serve.

The onion may be put in raw if cut fine, provided the tomatoes are stewed longer, which is desirable, and instead of bread, 2 table-spoonsful of flour might be mixed with a piece of butter as large as a turkey's egg, and stirred in half an hour before dinner.

Another way to stew Tomatoes.—Slice the tomatoes into a well-tinned stew-pan, seasoning them with pepper and salt; place bits of butter over the top. Put on the lid close, and stew gently for about 20 minutes. After this stir them frequently, letting them stew until they arc well done. A spoonful or two of vinegar will be considered an improvement by many. Excellent with roast beef or mutton.

To bake.—Slice them into a baking-dish; season, put butter over in bits, and strew bread-crumbs on the top. Bake them for about three-quarters of an hour in a moderate oven.

To stuff.—Cut them in halves and hollow out the centre; take whatever cold meat may be at hand, either chicken, partridge, or hare, with ham, &c, onions, fine herbs, crumbs of bread, and form a forcemeat ball, with beaten eggs; fill up the centres of the tomatoes, and let them stew gently in any gravy; before serving up, pass them over with a salamander or hot iron.

Portuguese way.—A favorite mode of dressing them in Portugal, where they are largely grown, is, to stew them along with rice and onions in strong brown gravy; the rice forming the greater portion of the dish. There are also various other ways employed throughout the Continent, but garlic should never be added, as it destroys the delicacy of the tomato.

Eggs and Tomatoes.—Peel the skins from 12 large tomatoes; put 4 oz. of butter in a frying pan; add some salt, pepper, and a little chopped onion; fry it a few minutes—add the tomatoes and chop them while frying; when nearly done, break in 6 eggs, stir them quickly, and serve them up.

Ochra and Tomatoes, or Gumbo.—Take an equal quantity of each; let the ochras be young; slice them and skin the tomatoes; put them into a pan without water, adding a lump of butter, an onion chopped fine, some pepper and salt, and stew them one hour.

A Spanish Dish.—Peel the skins from ripe tomatoes; put them in a pan with a table-spoonful of melted butter, some pepper, salt, and an onion chopped fine. Shred cold meat or fowl; add it to the tomatoes, and fry it sufficiently.

To keep Tomatoes a year.—Take half a bushel, skin and boil them well, then add a tea-cupful of salt, a table-spoonful of black pepper, one table-spoonful of Cayenne, an ounce of cloves, an ounce of mace. Mix well, and put them in jars, and run mutton suet over them, and tie them up with strong paper or buckskin, and they will keep well, free from mould and acidity.

ASPARAGUS.

To boil Asparagus.—Scrape clean the stalks, and throw them into cold water; tie them in bundles of about 20 each, with tape, and cut the stalks even. Put them into boiling water, with a handful of salt, and boil half an hour, or until they are tender at the stalk. Having toasted a round of bread, dip it into the water in which the asparagus were boiled, lay them upon the toast, the white ends outwards each way; and serve with melted butter.

Asparagus dressed like Green Peas.—This is a convenient mode of dressing asparagus, when it is too small and green to make a good appearance plainly boiled. Cut the points so far only as they are perfectly tender, in bits of equal size, not more than the third of an inch in length; wash them very clean, and throw them into plenty of boiling water, with the usual quantity of salt and a morsel of soda. When they are tolerably tender, which will be in from 10 to 12 minutes, drain them well, and spread them on a clean cloth; fold it over them, wipe them gently, and when they are quite dry put them into a clean stew-pan with a good slice of butter, which should be just dissolved before the asparagus is added; stew them in this over a brisk fire, shaking them often, for 8 or 10 minutes; dredge in about a small tea-spoonful of flour, and add half that quantity of white sugar; then pour in boiling water to nearly cover the asparagus, and boil it rapidly until but little liquid remains; stir in the beaten yolks of 2 eggs, heap the asparagus high in a dish and serve it very hot. The sauce should adhere entirely to the vegetable.

MUSHROOMS.

Cooks should be perfectly acquainted with the different sorts of things called by this name by ignorant people, as the dish of many persons has been occasioned by carelessly using the poisonous kinds.[*]

The *eatable mushrooms* at first appear very small and of a round form on a little stalk. They grow very fast, and the upper part and stalk are white. As the size increases, the under part gradually opens, and shows a fringed fur of a very fine salmon color, which continues more or less till the mushroom has gained some size, and then turns to a dark brown. These marks should be attended to, and likewise whether the skin can be easily parted from the edges and middle. Those that have a white or yellow fur should be carefully avoided, though many of them have the same smell, but not so strong, as the right sort.

To stew Mushrooms.—The large buttons are best for this purpose, and the small flaps while the fur is still red. Rub the buttons with salt and a bit of flannel; cut out the fur, and take off the skin from the others; put them into a stew-pan with a little lemon juice, pepper, salt, and a small piece of fresh butter, and let the whole simmer slowly till done; then put a small bit a butter and flour, with 2 spoonsful of cream; give them one boil, and serve with sippets of bread.

To stew Mushrooms—an easy way.—Cut off that part of the stem that grows under ground, wash them carefully, and take the skin from the top. Put them into a stew-pan with some salt but no water; stew them till tender, and thicken with a table-spoonful of butter, mixed with one of browned flour.

To broil Mushrooms.—The largest are the best. Have a clear cinder fire; make the gridiron hot, and rub the bars with suet to prevent the mushrooms from sticking; place them also on the gridiron with their stalks upwards; sprinkle them slightly with salt, and a good shake of pepper, and serve them on a hot dish, with a little cold butter under and over them. When they begin to steam they are sufficiently done.

* We do not believe that mushrooms are nutritive; every one knows they are often dangerously indigestible; therefore the rational epicure will be content with extracting the flavor from them, which is obtained in the almost perfection in good mushroom catsup.—*Dr. Kitchiner.*

SALADS, MACARONI, ETC.

Different kinds of Salads—Salad dressing—Summer Salad Winter Salad—Vegetable Salads—French—Italian—Spanish—Vinaigrette—Chicken—Tomatoes en Salade—Coldslaw—Radishes—Cucumbers—To dress Macaroni—Milonese—à Eitalienne Pàti de Macaroni—Vermicelli—Stewed Cheese—Roast Cheese—Welsh Rabbit.

SALAD.— The herbs and vegetables for a salad cannot be too freshly gathered; they should be carefully cleared from insects and washed with scrupulous nicety; they are better when not prepared until near the time of sending them to table, and should not be sauced until the instant before they are served. Tender lettuces, of which the outer leaves should be stripped away, mustard and cress, young radishes, and occasionally chives or small green onions (when the taste of a party is in favor of these last) are the usual ingredients of summer salads, Half grown cucumbers sliced thin, and mixed with them, are a favorite addition with many persons. In England it is customary to cut the lettuces extremely fine; the French, who object to the *flavor of the knife*, which they fancy this mode imparts, break them small instead. Young celery alone, sliced and dressed with a rich salad mixture is excellent: it is still in some families served thus always with roast fowls.

Beet-root, baked or boiled, blanched endive, small salad-herbs which are easily raised at any time of the year, celery, and hardy lettuces, with any ready-dressed vegetable, will supply salads through the winter. Cucumber vinegar is an agreeable addition to these.

In *summer salads* the mixture must not be poured upon the lettuce or vegetables used in the salad, but be left at the bottom, to be stirred up when wanted, as thus preserving the crispness of the lettuce.

In *winter salads*, however, the reverse of this proceeding must be adopted, as thus: the salad of endive, celery, beet, and other roots being cut ready for dressing, then pour the mixture upon the ingredients, and stir them well up, so that every portion may receive its benefit.

In doing this, it should likewise be recollected that the spoon and fork should always be of wood, and of sufficient size to stir up the vegetables in large quantities.*

Salad dressing.—For a salad of moderate size pound very smoothly the yolks of two hard boiled eggs with a small tea spoonful of unmade mustard, half as much sugar in fine powder, and a salt-spoonful of salt. Mix gradually with these a small cup of cream, or the same quantity of very pure oil, and two table-spoonsful of vinegar. More salt and acid can be added at pleasure; but the latter usually predominates too much in English salads. A few drops of Cayenne vinegar will improve this receipt.

Hard yolks of eggs, 2; unmade mustard, 1 small tea-spoonful; sugar, half as much; salt, 1 salt-spoonful; cream or oil, small cupful; vinegar, 2 table-spoonsful.

Obs. 1.—To some tastes a tea-spoonful or more of eschalot vinegar would be an acceptable addition to this sauce, which may be otherwise varied in numberless ways. Cucumber-vinegar may be substituted for other, and small quantities of soy, cavice, essence of anchovies, or catsup may in turn be used to flavor the compound. The salad bowl too may be rubbed with a cut clove of garlic, to give the whole composition a very slight flavor of it. The eggs should be boiled for fifteen minutes, and allowed to become quite cold always before they are pounded, or the mixture will not be smooth: if it should curdle, which it will sometimes do, if not carefully made, add to it the yolk of a very fresh unboiled egg.

Obs. 2.—As we have before had occasion to remark, garlic, when very sparingly and judiciously used, imparts a remarkably fine savor to a sauce or gravy, and neither a strong nor a coarse cue, as it does when used in larger quantities. The veriest morsel (or, as the French call it, a mere *soupcon*) of the root is sufficient to give this agreeable piquancy, but unless the proportion be extremely small, the effect will be quite different. The Italians dress their salads upon a round of delicately toasted bread, which is rubbed with garlic, saturated with oil, and sprinkled with Cayenne, before it is laid into the bowl: they also eat the bread thus prepared, but with less of oil, and untoasted often before their meals, as a digestor.

French Salad dressing.—Stir a saltspoonful of salt and half as much pepper into a large spoonful of oil, and when the salt is dissolved, mix with them four additional spoonsful of oil, and pour the whole over the salad; let it be *well* turned, and then add a couple of spoonsful of vinegar; mix the whole thoroughly and serve it without delay. The salad should not be, dressed in this way until the instant before it is wanted for table: the proportions of salt and pepper can be increased at pleasure, and common, or cucumber-vinegar may be substituted for the tarragon, which, however is more frequently used in France than any other.

Another Salad dressing.—Boil two eggs ten minutes, and put them into cold water, to harden and cool; then take out the yolks, and rub them through a coarse sieve into a basin; add two table-spoonsful of olive oil, a tea-spoonful of salt, the same quantity of mustard, half the quantity of ground black pepper, a tea-spoonful of soy or essence of anchovies, and two table-spoonsful of vinegar: incorporate the whole, and pour this sauce down the side of the salad-bowl, or keep it in an incorporator. The whites of the eggs will serve to garnish the salad.

Summer Salad.—Wash very clean one or two heads of fine lettuce, divide it, let it lie some time in cold water; drain and dry it in a napkin, and cut it small before serving. Mustard and cresses, sorrel and young onions, may be added.

Winter Salad.—Wash very clean one or two heads of endive, some heads of celery, some mustard and cresses; cut them all small, add a little shredded red cabbage, some slices of boiled beet-root, an onion, if the flavor is not disliked; mix them together with salad sauce. In spring, add radishes, and also garnish the dish with them.

Vegetable Salads made of roots which have been boiled, also make good winter salads, amongst which *potato* and *beet-root salads* are perhaps the best. Cut the roots into thin slices, season them with pepper and salt, and pour over them the salad mixture, to which may be added, if the flavor be not did approved, a few slices of raw onion.

French Salad.—Chop 3 anchovies, a shalot, and some parsley small, put them into a bowl with 2 table-spoonsful of vinegar, 1 of oil, a little mustard, and salt. When well mixed, add by degrees some cold roast or boiled meat in very thin slices; put in a few at a time, not exceeding 2 or 3 inches long. Shake them in the seasoning, and then put more; cover the bowl close, and let the salad be prepared 3 hours before it is to be eaten.

Italian Salad is made by picking the white portion of a cold fowl from the bones in small flakes, piling it in the centre of a dish, and pouring a salad mixture over, enriched with cream; make a wall around with salad of any kind, lading the whites of eggs, cut into rings, on the top in a chain.

Spanish Salad.—Take whatever salad can be got, wash it in many waters, rinse it in a small net, or in napkins, till nearly dry, chop up onions and tarragon, take a bowl, put in equal quantities of vinegar and water, a tea-spoonful of pepper and salt, and four times as much oil as vinegar and water; mix the same well together; take care never to put the lettuce into the sauce till the moment the salad is wanted, or it loses all its crispness and becomes sodden.

For Vinaigrette.—Take any kind of cold meat, chop it finely, and lay it in a dish; chop the whites of the eggs employed for the salad very finely with small onions; add any kind of herb, and pickled cucumbers, all chopped finely; make a garnish round the meat, serve it with salad mixture, but do not stir it together, as it would spoil the appearance of the dish, which looks very pretty with the eggs and herbs in a ring.

Chicken Salad.—Boil a chicken that weighs not more than a pound and a half. When very tender, take it up, cut it in small strips; then take 6 or 7 fine white heads of celery, scrape and wash it; cut the white part small, in pieces about three-quarters of an inch long, mix it with the meat of the fowl, and just before the salad is sent in, pour a dressing made in the following way, over it.

Boil 4 eggs hard; rub their yolks to a smooth paste with 2 table-spoonsful of olive oil; 2 tea-spoonsful of made mustard; 1 tea-spoonful of salt, and 1 tea-cupful of strong vinegar.

Place the delicate leaves of the celery around the edges of the dish.

White-heart lettuce may be used instead of celery.

Any other salad dressing may be used, if preferred.

Tomatoes en Salade.—These are now often served merely sliced, and dressed like cucumbers, with salt, pepper, oil, and vinegar.

For Winter use.—Late in the season take tomatoes not too ripe, cut them into thick slices, salt them lightly in a flat dish, sprinkling the salt over them as you cut them. Pour off the water; put them in ajar, strewing black and Cayenne pepper through them and a few slices of onion, 2 wineglassfuls of sweet oil, a few blades of mace, and vinegar enough to cover them up tight to exclude the air.

Coldslaw.—Shave as fine as possible a hard head of white cabbage, put it in a salad bowl, and pour over it the usual salad dressing.

Another way is, to cut the cabbage head in two, shave ill finely, put it in a stew-pan with half a tea-cupful of butter, a tea-spoonful of salt, two table-spoonsful of vinegar, and a salt-spoonful of pepper; cover the stew-pan, and set over a gentle fire for five minutes, shaking it occasionally. When thoroughly heated, serve it as a salad.

Radishes.—Radishes should always be freshly gathered; let them lie in cold water one hour before serving, then cut off all their leaves and almost all the stalk, serve them in glasses half filled with water, or on a plate.

Shalots or Green Onions are sometimes served and eaten in the same way.

Dressed Cucumbers.—Pare and slice them very thin, strew a little fine salt over them, and when they have stood a few minutes drain off the water, by raising one side of the dish, and letting it flow to the other; pour it away, strew more salt, and a moderate seasoning of pepper on them, add two or three table-spoonsful of the purest salad-oil, and turn the cucumbers well, that the whole may receive a portion of it; then pour over them from one to three dessertspoonsful of Chili vinegar, and a little common, should it be needed; turn them into a clean dish and serve them.

To dress Macaroni.—Wash and drain as much macaroni as you desire for dinner; put it on to boil in tepid water. When it is soft enough to pass a fork through, take it off, drain it through a cullender, wipe out the skillet, and return it immediately back again. Then add milk enough to half cover it, salt and red pepper to your taste, a piece of butter as large as a turkey's egg, and grated cheese as plentifully as you please; stew it all together, while stirring it for 5 or 10 minutes; then throw it out into a dish, cover the top with grated bread crumbs, and set it in the oven for a few minutes to brown on the top. If left long in the oven it will dry up and become tough and unpalatable.

Macaroni Milanese.—Throw the maccaroni in boiling water with some salt in it. Let it have plenty of room and be well covered with water. Let it boil 25 minutes. Drain it in a cullender; then put it in a deep dish in alternate layers of macaroni and grated cheese; lay on the top slices of fresh butter; pour over it milk and cream enough to cover the whole, and place the dish in an oven where it can cook at the top and bottom equally. In 15 or 20 minutes it will be done. Serve it up immediately. Too much fire will make it dry.

Macaroni ā L' Italienne.—Take one quarter of a pound of macaroni, boil it in water till tender; thicken half a pint of milk with flour and a small bit of butter; add 2 table-spoonsful of cream, half a tea-spoonful of mustard, a little white pepper, salt, and cayenne. Stir into this half a pound of grated cheese; boil all together a few minutes; add the macaroni; make all quite hot, and serve. This is the mode adopted at the best tables in Florence.

Pâte de Macaroni.—Stew some macaroni in butter and water or broth, strain it, cut it into pieces, and lay it at the bottom of the dish, adding ham balls, made of ham pounded in a mortar, and blended with butter; then have ready any kind of game, boned and filleted, sweetbread cut into dice, and mushrooms, all stewed in good rich sauce; place a layer upon the macaroni, then another layer of meat, and until the pie is filled, add to it equal quantities of cream and gravy, cover it with a paste, and bake it, or omit the paste, and stew it before the fire in a Dutch oven. The macaroni may be mixed with grated Parmesan or rich old cheese.

Another mode.—Swell 4 oz. of pipe macaroni in milk, with a large onion. Put a layer at the bottom of a pie-dish, with some bits of butter and scraped cheese sprinkled lightly over. Cover the whole with a well-seasoned beef-steak, cut small and thin, then some more macaroni, and then another layer of beef steak; cover the whole with macaroni, pieces of butter, and grated cheese, instead of crust. Bake in a slow oven.

Cold Macaroni.—If already dressed, may be warmed in any kind of broth, letting it simmer gently upon a slow fire, with the yolks of 2 eggs to thicken; after which it should be put into the oven in a mould covered with crumbs of bread: or, *if undressed,* it may be made by leaving it over night in broth, and then proceeding with it as above.

Vermicelli—Is of the same substance as macaroni, but made much smaller, and frequently put into meat soups, as giving them additional richness; but it is, in our country, too sparingly used. To be well made the soup should be thickened with it, and for that purpose it is preferable to macaroni.

Semolina—Is of the same material, but made into small grains, which more easily thicken the soup into which it is mixed: it can also be made into an excellent pudding with eggs and milk, using it instead of flour.

It should be observed, as a general rule, that in using any of the Italian pastes—unless they should be sweetened—old. or Parmesan cheese should always form part of the dish, in the proportion of one-half the quantity to that of the paste.

CHEESE.

Stewed Cheese.—Slice thinly or grate 2 ounces of fat cheese into a sauce-pan; add a little ale or porter, and set before a clear fire, occasionally stirring them until the cheese is entirely melted. If the cheese be not very fat, butter may be added.

Or: grate cheese into a sauce-pan, melt it, and stir in a little cream and a well-beaten egg; and, if necessary, a little butter.

To Roast Cheese.—Mix two ounces grated cheese with the yolk of an egg, two ounces of grated bread, and about an ounce of butter; beat them in a mortar, with mustard, pepper, and salt, to a paste, which spread thickly on toast, and warm and lightly brown it in a Dutch oven.

Cheese Toast.—Grate thickly over well-buttered toast, good Cheshire cheese, and lightly brown it before the fire.

Welsh Rabbit.—Cut bread half an inch thick, toast it on both sides very lightly, and cut off the crust; then cut a slice of fat cheese without rind, not quite so large as the toast, upon which lay the cheese in a toaster before a clear fire: watch it lest it burn or get hard, and when the cheese is thoroughly melted, remove from the fire and season with mustard, pepper, and salt. Some persons prefer the bread toasted on one side only

---

Devilled Biscuits.—Butter captain's biscuits on both sides, and pepper them well; make a slice of cheese into a paste with made mustard, and lay it on upon one side; sprinkle Cayenne pepper on the top, and send them to be grilled. This may be varied by the addition of chopped anchovies, or the essence, diavolo paste, or Chetney.

* There is a Spanish proverb which says, "To make a good salad, four persons are wanted,—a spendthrift for oil, a miser for vinegar, a counsellor for salt and a madman to stir it all up."

EGGS AND OMELETTES.

To Choose Eggs—To Keep for Winter—To Boil—Poach— Cupped— Scrambled—Œufs Brouilliés—Soufflé—Omelettes—Savory, or Ragoût Eggs.

To Choose Eggs.—In choosing eggs hold them to the light: if they are clear, they are fresh; if they are thick, they are stale; if they have a black spot attached to the shell, they are worthless. Eggs should be new, or not more than 24 hours old, when they are stored, else their flavor cannot be relied on. The safest mode of choosing them is by holding them to the light of a candle.

Unless an egg is perfectly fresh it is unfit for any purpose.[*] You may try the freshness of eggs by putting them in a pan of cold water. Those that sink the soonest are the freshest. Eggs may be preserved a short time by putting them in a jar of salt or lime water, with the small ends downwards. The salt should not afterwards be used. They may be preserved several months by greasing them all over with melted mutton suet, and wedging them close together in a box of bran. The small ends always downwards.

To Keep Eggs for Winter Use.—Pour a full gallon of boiling water on two quarts of quick lime and half a pound of salt; when cold, mix it into an ounce of cream of tartar. The day following put in the eggs. After the lime has been stirred well into the boiling water, a large part of it will settle at the bottom of the vessel, on which the eggs will remain. Keep them covered with the liquor, and they will keep for 2 years.

To Boil Eggs to eat in the Shells, or for Salads.—The fresher laid, the better: put them into boiling water; if you like the white just set, about 2 minutes boiling is enough; a new-laid egg will take a little more; if you wish the yolk to be set, it will take 3, and to boil it hard for a salad, 10 minutes.

Obs.—A new-laid egg will require boiling longer than a stale one, by half a minute.

Tin machines for boiling eggs on the breakfast table are sold by the iron-mongers, which perform the process very regularly: in 4 minutes the white is just set.

Poached Eggs.—The beauty of a poached egg is for the yolk to be seen blushing through the white, which should only be just sufficiently hardened, to form a transparent veil for the egg.

Have some boiling water in a tea-kettle; pass as much of it through a clean cloth as will half fill a stew-pan; break the egg into a cup, and when the water boils, remove the stew-pan from the stove, and gently slip the egg into it; it must stand till the white is set; then put it over a very moderate fire, and as soon as the water boils, the egg is ready; take it up with a slice, and neatly round off the ragged edges of the white; send them up on bread toasted on one side only, with or without butter.

To poach Eggs in the Frying-pan.—Put very little butter, oil, or top-pot into the frying-pan: break the eggs gently into a deep cup, of the size the egg is to be of, sometimes smaller, sometimes larger; with a quick slight turn of the hand, turn the cup over with the egg into the pan, and leave the cup upon it, and continue to turn over the cups till all the eggs are put in; the fire must be very slow: when the first egg has taken, raise the cup a little to ascertain it: they must be done very slowly, otherwise the under part will be over-done: dress them over parsley, spinach, or on toasted bread.

Cupped Eggs.—Put a spoonful of very nice high-seasoned brown gravy into each cup; set the cups in a sauce-pan of boiling water; when the gravy heats, drop a fresh egg into each cup; take off the sauce-pan, and cover it close till the eggs are nicely and tenderly cooked; dredge them with very fine mace, or nutmeg and salt; serve them in a hot-water plate, covered with a napkin.

Scrambled Eggs.—Beat seven or eight eggs quite light, and throw them into a clean frying-pan with a small quantity of butter and a little salt. Stir them carefully until they are well thickened, and turn them out on a hot dish, without permitting any portion of them to adhere to the frying-pan. This dish is excellent with a trimming of stewed tomatoes.

Œufs Brouillés.—Break 4 or 6 eggs; beat them and put them into a saucepan with a piece of butter, a little salt, and a spoonful of sauce or gravy, which makes the eggs softer; stir them over the fire until sufficiently thick; serve on a plate garnished with toasted bread. To eggs dressed this way, ham, mushrooms, &c., minced, may be added. The difference between this and an omelette is, that an omelette is compact and turns out smooth, whereas *œufs brouilles* are less done, and are therefore broken.

In Ireland, where it is in general use, it is usually served upon hot buttered toast, and is there called *"buttered eggs."* It is also very common in France, where it is usually served for breakfast.

Or:—Butter a dish well, sprinkle it with salt, then break the eggs very carefully so as not to disturb the yolk; add a little more salt and some white pepper; melt a small quantity of butter, pour it gently over, with 1 or 2 spoonsful of cream. Put the dish over a slow fire, and finish the eggs by covering them with a red-hot shovel.

Soufflé Française.—Put into a stew-pan 1 oz. of butter; when melted, add 2 table-spoonsful of flour; stir them well over the fire, so that the flour be thoroughly cooked, but not colored; add by degrees a wineglass of boiling cream, and four times that quantity of boiling milk; work it quite smooth, take it off the fire, add 4 yolks of eggs, sugar to palate, a grain of salt, and a table-spoonful of orange-flower water; whip up strongly the whites of 8 eggs, mix them lightly in the batter put the whole into a soufflé-dish, and bake for an hour.

The flavor of this soufflée may be varied according to fancy, omitting the orange-flower water, and substituting either vanilla, curacoa, noyeau, maraschino, chocolate, coffee, &c.

OMELETTE.

Omelettes.—Eggs[*] may be dressed in a multiplicity of ways put are seldom, in any form, more relished than in a well-made and expeditiously served omelette. This may be plain, or seasoned with minced herbs, and a very little eschalot, when the last is liked, and is then called an *"Omelette aux fines herbes;"* or it may be mixed with minced ham, or grated cheese; in any case, it should be light, thick, full-tasted, and *fried only on one side*; if turned in the pan, as it frequently is, it will at once be flattened and rendered tough. Should the slight rawness which is sometimes found in the middle of the inside, when the omelette is made in the French way, be objected to, a heated shovel, or a salamander, may be held over it for an instant, before it is folded on the dish. The pan for frying it should be quite small; for, if it be composed of 4 or 5 eggs only, and then put into a large one, it will necessarily spread over it and be thin, which would render it more like a pancake than an omelette; the only partial remedy for this, when a pan of proper size cannot be had, is to raise the handle of it high, and to keep the opposite side close down to the fire, which will confine the eggs into a smaller space. No gravy should ever be poured into the dish with it, and indeed, if properly made, it will require none. Lard must not be used for omelettes.

Four eggs will make a very pretty sized omelette, but the number of eggs must of course depend on the size required. If sweet herbs be put in, a good deal of parsley should form part; tarragon gives a high flavor, and chives or shalots are not unfrequently used, but care should be taken that the flavor should not supersede that of the other ingredients.

Omelettes are judiciously varied by mixing minced ham or tongue with them, when served at supper or as a side-dish at dinner; but when intended for the breakfast table, it is more delicate to make them of eggs alone.

A Common Omelette.—From 4 to 8 very fresh eggs may be used for this, according to the sized dish required. Half a dozen will generally be sufficient. Break them singly and carefully; clear them, or when they are sufficiently whisked pour them through a sieve, and resume the beating until they are very light. Add to them from half to a whole tea-spoonful of salt, and a seasoning of pepper. Dissolve in a small frying-pan a couple of ounces of butter, pour in the eggs, and as soon as the omelette is well risen and firm throughout, slide it on to a hot dish, fold it together like a turnover, and serve it *immediately.* From 5 to 7 minutes will fry it.

An Omelette Soufflée.—Separate as they are broken, the whites from the yolks of 6 fine fresh eggs; beat these last thoroughly, first by themselves and then with 4 table-spoonsful of dry white-sifted sugar, and the rind of half a lemon grated on a fine grater. Whisk the whites to a solid froth, and just before the omelette is poured into the pan, mix them well, but lightly, with the yolks. Put 4 oz. of fresh butter into a very small delicately clean omelette, or frying-pan, and as soon as it is all dissolved, add the eggs and stir them round, that they may absorb it entirely. When the under side is just set, turn the omelette into a well-buttered dish, and send it to a tolerably brisk oven. From 5 to 10 minutes will bake it; and it must be served the *instant* it is taken out; carried, indeed, as quickly as possible to table from the oven. It will have risen to a great height, but will sink and become heavy in a very short space of time: if sugar be sifted over it, let it be done with the utmost expedition.

Eggs, 6; sugar, 4 table-spoonsful; rind, half a lemon; butter, 4 oz.: omelette baked, 5 to 10 minutes.

Savory, or Ragoút Eggs.—Boil the eggs hard, as for salad, put them into cold water, remove the shells, cut them into halves, and take out the yolks, keeping the white halves unbroken; then beat up the yolks in a mortar, with forcemeat, with lean ham in it; fill the halves with this mixture, fry them lightly, and serve with good brown gravy over them, either with or without slices of ham or bacon. Or, beat up the yolks with anchovy paste, or shred ham, fill the whites, and serve cold as a supper dish.

* Bought eggs ought always to be suspected; therefore, let an earthen pan be kept with charcoal or lime-water in the pantry to put them in. The longer they are kept in it, the better they will be, as these waters destroy must, and even corruption.

* They reckon 685 ways of dressing eggs in the French kitchen: we trust our more limited number will be sufficient for Americans. A *good* egg, cooked, in almost any way, or *uncooked,* is good and nutritious food.

PASTRY.

Directions for making Paste—Baking Pies—Glazing Pastry—French Puff Paste—Good Puff Paste—Light Paste—Suet Paste—Seasoning for Raised Pies—Meat Pies—Modern Potato Pastry—Beef-steak Pie—Veal —Mutton—Pork—Ham—Sea-Pie—Chicken—Giblet—Partridge— Venison—Cold Pies—Vol au Vent—Oyster Patties—Chicken Patties— Mince Pies—Fruit Pies—Tarts—Apple Pie—Pumpkin—Squash— Custard—Potato—Peach—Cocoa-nut—Cheese Cakes—Puffs.

THE art of making paste requires a good memory, practice, and dexterity; for, it is principally from the method of mixing the various ingredients of which it is composed, that paste acquires its good or bad qualities.

Before making paste, wash the hands in hot water; touch the paste as little as possible, and roll it but little; the less the better. If paste be much wetted it will be tough.

A marble slab is better than a board to make paste on: both, together with the rolling-pin, cutters, and tins, should be kept very clean; as the least dust or hard paste left on either will spoil the whole.

The coolest part of the house and of the day should be chosen for the process during warm weather.

Flour for the finest paste should be dried and sifted, as should pounded white sugar.

Butter should be added to paste in very small pieces, unless otherwise directed.

If fresh butter be not used, break salt butter into pieces, wash it well in spring water, to cleanse it from salt, squeeze it carefully, and dry it upon a soft cloth. Fresh butter should also be well worked to get out the buttermilk.

After the butter has been pressed and worked well with a wooden knife on the paste-board, press it very lightly with a clean, soft cloth, to absorb the moisture. If good fresh butter is used, it will require very little if any working.

Lard is sometimes used instead of butter, but the saving is of very trifling importance, when it is considered that although lard will make paste light, it will neither be of so good color or flavor as when made with butter.

Dripping, especially from beef, when very sweet and clean, is often used for kitchen pies: and is, in this instance, a good substitute for butter, lard, &c.

In hot weather the butter should be broken into pieces, and put into spring water, or into ice; but, on no account, put the paste into ice, else the butter in it will harden, and in baking, melt, and separate from the paste.

The same thing happens in winter, when the butter has not been sufficiently worked, and the paste is rather soft; for, though the season be favorable to the making of paste, care must be taken to work the butter sufficiently.

In winter, paste should be made very firm, because the butter is then so; in summer, the paste should be made soft, as the butter is then the same.

It is important to work up paste lightly and gradually into an uniform body—no strength nor pressure being used.

It is necessary to lightly flour both sides of paste when you roll it, in order to prevent its turning grey in baking; but, if much flour be sprinkled on it, the paste will not be clear.

Attention to the rolling out is most important to make light puff-paste; if it be too light, it may be rolled out once or twice more than directed; as the folding mainly causes it to rise high and even.

Be sure, *invariably*, to roll puff-paste *from you*. Those who are not practiced in making puff-paste, should work the butter in, by breaking it into small pieces, and covering the paste rolled out; dredge it lightly with flour, fold over the sides and ends, roll it out very thin, add the remainder of the butter, and fold and roll as before.

To ensure lightness, paste should be set in the oven as soon after it is made as possible; on this account, the paste should not be begun to be made till the oven is half heated, which sometimes occupies an hour. If paste be left 20 minutes on more before it is baked, it will become dull and heavy.

Paste should be light, without being greasy; and baked of a fine color, without being burnt; therefore, to ensure good baking, requires attention.

Puff-paste requires a brisk oven; a moderate one will best bake pies and tarts, puddings and biscuits. Regulation of heat, according to circumstances, is the main point in baking.

If the oven be too hot, the paste, besides being burned, will not rise well; and if it be too slack, the paste will be soddened, not rise, and want color. Raised pies require the quickest oven.

When fruit pies are baked in iron ovens, the syrup is apt to boil out of them; to prevent this, set a few thin bricks on the bottom of the oven before it is seated; but this will not be requisite, if the oven have a stone bottom.

Tart-tins, cake-moulds, and dishes, should be well buttered before baking; articles to be baked on sheets should be placed on buttered paper.

Directions for Baking Pies.—Before you put any thing to bake, be sure the oven is quite clean, for if the juice or gravy of any thing which is baking should boil over into the oven, or anything dirty has been in the oven, it will give a disagreeable taste to whatever is baked in it. A cook should therefore be careful to sweep and clean her oven carefully out with a damp cloth, before she lights her fire, or before it is too hot to do so, and let it dry before she closes the door tight. All pies must be attended to while cooking, to see that the juice does not boil over, for if it does, it will make a steam in the oven, which will spoil your crust, by making it heavy, and make the pie appear to be done, before it is well warmed. After it has been in the oven about half an hour, at furthest it must be looked to, and turned, or it may be spoiled, by burning at one part and not cooking at another.

If you should find the juice of a pie run over, you must take out your pie, raise the crust at one end, and pour out some of the juice, which save, and pour again into the pie when it is done, if there is room, and if not, send it up with the pie in a boat, or sauce-tureen.

To Glaze or Ice Pastry.—The fine yellow glaze appropriate to meat pies is given with beaten yolk of egg, which should be laid on with a paste brush, or a small bunch of feathers: if a lighter color be wished for, whisk the whole of the egg together or mix a little milk with the yolk.

The best mode of icing fruit-tarts before they are sent to the oven is, to moisten the paste with cold water, to sift sugar thickly upon it, and to press it lightly on with the hand; but when a *whiter* icing is preferred, the pastry must be drawn from the oven when nearly baked, and brushed with white of egg, whisked to a froth; then well covered with the sifted sugar, and sprinkled with a few drops of water before it is put in again: this glazing answers also very well, though it takes a slight color, if used before the pastry is baked.

Feuilletage, or Fine French Puff Paste.—This, when made by a good French cook, is the perfection of rich light crust, and will rise in the oven from one to six inches in height; but some practice is, without doubt, necessary to accomplish this. In summer it is a great advantage to have ice at hand, and to harden the butter over it before it is used; the paste also in the intervals of rolling is improved by being laid on an oven-leaf over a vessel containing it. Take an equal weight of good butter free from the coarse salt which is found in some, and which is disadvantageous for this paste, and of fine dry, sifted flour; to each pound of these allow the yolks of a couple of eggs, and a small tea-spoonful of salt. Break a few small bits of the butter very lightly into the flour, put the salt into the centre, and pour on it sufficient water to dissolve it (we do not quite understand why the doing this should be better than mixing it with the flour, as in other pastes, but such is the method always pursued for it); add a little more water to the eggs, moisten the flour gradually, and make it into a *very* smooth paste, rather lithe in summer, and never *exceedingly* stiff, though the opposite fault, in an extreme, would render the crust unmanageable. Press, in a soft thin cloth, all the moisture from the remainder of the butter, and form it into a ball, but in doing this be careful not to soften it too much. Should it be in an unfit state for pastry, from the heat of the weather, put it into a basin, and set the basin in a pan of water mixed with plenty of salt and saltpetre, and let it remain in a cool place for an hour if possible, before it is used. When it is ready (and the paste should never be commenced until it be so), roll the crust out square,[*] and of sufficient size to enclose the butter, flatten this a little upon it in the centre, and then fold the crust well over it, and roll it out thin as lightly as possible, after having dredged the board and paste, roller with a little flour: this is called giving it *one turn*. Then fold it in three, give it another turn, and set it aside, where it will be very cool, for a few minutes; give it two more turns in the same way, rolling it each time very lightly, but of equal thickness, and to the full length that it will reach, taking always especial care that the butter shall not break through the paste. Let it again be set aside to become cold; and after it has been twice more rolled and folded in three, give it a half-turn, by folding it once only, and it will be ready for use.

Equal weight of the finest flour and good butter; to each pound of these, the yolks of two eggs, and a small salt-spoonful of salt: six and half turns to be given to the paste.

Good Puff Paste.—Take 1 lb. of flour, sift it; 1 lb. of butter, and divide it into 4 equal parts; weigh ¼ lb. of flour to dust with. Rub one of the quarters of butter into the pound of flour, and mix up with a very little very cold water; roll out 3 times, adding each time a quarter of butter, and dusting each time with flour. When you cut off from the large roll of dough a piece for one pie, roll out the piece you cut off very thin, and dust it with flour, double it in folds and roll it the thickness of your crust.

Very Light Paste.—Mix the flour and water together, roll the paste out, and lay bits of butter upon it. Then beat up the white of an egg, and brush it all over the paste before it is folded; repeat this when rolling out, and adding the butter each time till the whole of the white of egg is used. It will make the paste very flaky.

For Tarts and Cheesecakes.—Beat the white of an egg to a strong froth; then mix it with as much water as will make three-quarters of a pound of fine flour into a very stiff paste: roll it very thin, then lay the third part of half a pound of butter upon it in little bits; dredge it with some flour left out at first, and roll it up tight. Roll it out again, and put the same proportion of butter; and so proceed till all be worked up.

Family Pie Paste.—Rub half a pound of butter into a pound of flour, and add water enough to knead it thoroughly.

Another common proportion is half a pound of butter to a pound and a half of flour.

Beef Dripping Paste.—Rub half a pound of clarified dripping into one pound of flour, work it into a stiff paste with water, and roll it twice or thrice. This crust is best eaten hot.

Suet Paste.—Rub well with half a pound of fresh beef suet, chopped as finely as possible, three-quarters of a pound of flour, and half a tea-spoonful of salt; make it into a stiff paste with cold water, work it well, beat it with the rolling-pin, and roll it out two or three times. This paste answers for any kind of boiled fruit pudding.

Potato Paste.—Mash 16 ounces of boiled potatoes, while they are warm, then rub them between the hands, together with 12 ounces of flour; when it is well mixed, and all looks like flour add half a tea-spoonful of salt, and, with a little cold water, make it into a stiff paste; beat and roll it out three or four times, making it very thin the last time. Lay over it black currant jam, raspberries, or any sort of preserve, rub the edges with water, roll it up like a bolster pudding, and boil it in a buttered and floured cloth for three or four hours. Serve it with a sweet sauce.

Paste for a Common Dumpling.—Rub into a pound of flour six ounces of butter, then work it into a paste with two well-beaten eggs and a little water. This paste may be baked, a large table-spoonful of pounded loaf sugar being added.

Raised Crust.—Melt, in one pint of water, one pound of fresh lard; weigh four pounds of flour, put it into a basin, and when the water and lard is hot, with a wooden spoon stir it by degrees amongst the flour. When well mixed, work it with the hands till it is a stiff paste, when it is fit for use.

Paste for Raised Pies.—Put two ounces of butter into a pint of boiling water, which mix, while hot, with three pounds of flour, into a strong but smooth paste; put it into a cloth to soak till near cold; then knead it, and raise it into the required shape.

To raise a pie well requires considerable practice; it is best done by putting one hand in the middle of the crust, and keeping the other close on the outside till you have worked it into the round or oval shape required: the lid is then to be rolled out. An unpracticed hand will, however, do better to roll the paste of a good thickness, and cut out a long piece for the circle of the pie, to be joined with egg as a hoop; then cut two pieces for the top and bottom: these are to be cemented with egg the bottom being brought out and pinched over: fill the pie, and pinch on the lid: or, if the crust be for a standing pie, line it with paper, fill it with bran, and bake it and the lid separately. The paste should be similarly joined with egg, if the pie be baked in a tin shape, when it should be put into the oven a few minutes after it is taken from the shape. In either case, wash the pie over with egg, and put on the ornaments before it is baked.

To make the ornaments, mix one ounce of sifted loaf sugar with half a pound of the above crust roll, and cut out.

Seasoning for Raised Pies.—Three pounds of salt dried and pounded, 3 oz. of white pepper, half oz. of Cayenne pepper, 2 oz. of cloves, 2 oz. of allspice, 1 oz. of basil, 1 oz. of marjoram, 1 oz. of thyme, 1 oz. of bay-leaf, 1 oz. of nutmeg, one and half oz. of mace.

Pound the spices and herbs by themselves, and sift through a fine sieve; then mix with the salt, and put away in a stoppered bottle: three-quarters of an ounce is sufficient for 1 lb. of farce, and half an ounce for 1 lb. of boned game.

Jelly for Meat or Raised Pies.—Take a quart of veal gravy dissolve 2 oz. of isinglass in a little of it; add the remainder with one-quarter pint of tarragon vinegar; boil all together for one-quarter of an hour. Clarify it with the whites of six eggs, then pass it through a bag.

Meat Pies, Patties &c.—There are few articles of cookery more generally liked than relishing pies, if properly made; and they may be formed of a great variety of things.

Raised Pies may be made of any kind of flesh, fish, fruit, or poultry, if baked in a wall of paste instead of a baking-dish: but they are generally eaten cold, and made so large and savory as to remain a long time before being consumed, for which reason they also bear the name of "standing pies." In making them the cook should always take care to have a good stock that will jelly, made from the bones and trimmings, to fill up the pie when it comes from the oven, and also that when cold there may be enough jelly. For want of this precaution pies become dry before they can be eaten. The materials are of course frequently varied, but the mode of preparation is so nearly the same as not to require the recital of more than a few prominent receipts.

Modern Potato Pasty; (an excellent family dish).—A tin mould of the construction shown in the plate, with a perforated moveable top, and a small valve to allow the escape of the steam, must be had for this pasty, which is an excellent family dish, and which may be varied in numberless ways. Arrange at the bottom of the mould from two to three pounds of mutton cutlets, freed, according to the taste, from all, or from the greater portion of the fat, then washed, lightly dredged on both sides with flour, and seasoned with salt and pepper, or Cayenne. Pour to them sufficient broth or water to make the gravy, and add to it at pleasure a table-spoonful of mushroom catsup or of Harvey's sauce. Have ready boiled, and *very* smoothly mashed, with about an ounce of butter, and a spoonful or two of milk or cream to each pound, as many good potatoes as will form a crust to the pasty of quite three inches thick; put the cover on the mould, and arrange these equally upon it, leaving them a little rough on the surface. Bake the pastry in a moderate oven from three-quarters of an hour to an hour and a quarter, according to its size and its contents. Pin a folded napkin neatly round the mould, before it is served, and have ready a hot dish to receive the cover, which must not be lifted off until after the pasty is on the table.

Chicken, or veal and oysters; delicate pork chops with a seasoning of sage and a little parboiled onion, or an eschalot or two finely minced; partridges or rabbits neatly carved, mixed with small mushrooms, and moistened with a little good stock, will all give excellent varieties of this dish, which may be made likewise with highly seasoned slices of salmon freed from the skin, sprinkled with fine herbs or intermixed with shrimps; clarified butter, rich veal stock, or good white wine, may be poured to them to form the gravy. To thicken this, a little flour should be dredged upon the fish before it is laid into the mould. Other kinds, such as cod, mackerel in fillets, salt fish (previously kept at the point of boiling until three parts done, then pulled into flakes, and put into the mould with hard eggs sliced, a little cream, flour, butter, Cayenne, and anchovy-essence, and baked with mashed parsneps on the top), will all answer well for this pasty. Veal, when used for it, should be well beaten first: sweetbreads, sliced, may be laid in with it.

For a pasty of moderate size, two pounds, or two and a half of meat, and from three to four of potatoes will be sufficient: a quarter-pint of milk or cream, two small tea-spoonsful of salt, and from one to two ounces of butter must be mixed up with these last.

Beef Steak Pie.—Choose steak that has been long hung, cut it into moderately-sized pieces, and trim off all skin or sinews; season them with pepper, salt, and minced shalot or onion, and lay them in the dish: put crust on the ledge and an inch below, cover with thick crust, and bake it about two hours. A tea-cupful of gravy or water may be put into the dish before the pie is baked, or some good gravy poured into it after it is taken from the oven.

A table-spoonful or two of mushroom catsup, or a flap mushroom, added to the steak, will greatly enrich this pie.

Beef Steak and Oyster Pie.—Prepare the steaks as above, and put layers of them and of oysters. Stew the liquor and beards of the latter with a bit of lemon-peel, mace, and a table-spoonful of walnut catsup. When the pie is baked, boll with the above 3 spoonsful of cream and 1 oz. of butter rubbed in flour; to which, however, many people object as injuring the savoriness of the pie; in which case, should any addition be required, a few spoonsful of beef gravy and port wine will answer the purpose. Strain it, and pour it into the dish: for a small pie a dozen of oysters will be sufficient, and the pie may be baked in a couple of hours.

Veal Pie.—Cut into steaks a loin or breast of veal, season them highly with pepper, salt, grated nutmeg, mace, and a little lemon-peel mixed; lay them into the bottom of a dish, and then a few slices of sweetbreads seasoned with the spices; add some oysters, forcemeat balls, and hard-boiled yolks of eggs, half a pint of white stock, and a table-spoonful of lemon pickle; put puff paste on the edge of the dish, and cover with the same; bake it for one hour.

Mutton Pie.—Cut the mutton into small slices, without bone; season it very well, and stew it with the fat also cut in pieces, putting in no water. When tender allow it to remain until cold; remove all the grease and fat very carefully; have some gravy made from the bones, add to it the strained gravy from the mutton, and a glass of port wine, but the wine may be omitted if the gravy be strong and highly seasoned. A minced shalot and button onions are good additions, and if the latter be pickled, their acidity will be an improvement. Put it into a dish, or into small pattypans, and bake it; if in pattypans, use puff paste. Mutton pies are better hot than cold.

The underdone part of a leg of mutton may be thus dressed; but the loin and kidneys are better suited for the purpose.

Raised Pork Pie.—Make a raised crust from 3 to 4 inches high; pare off the rind, and remove the bone from a loin of pork, cut it into chops, flatten them, and season them with chopped or powdered sage, black pepper, and salt, and pack them closely into the crust; then put on the top, and pinch the edge; brush the crust with yolk of egg, and bake 2 hours in a slow oven; when done, remove the lid, pour off the fat, and add some seasoned gravy.

Or:—The pork may be put into a dish, covered with crust and baked.

Or:—The pork may be cut into dice and seasoned.

When a log is killed, this pie may be made of the trimmings; but there should be no bone, as the meat must be packed closely, fat and lean alternately.

Raised Ham Pie.—Choose a small ham, soak it, boil it an hour, cut off the knuckle, then remove the rind, trim the ham, and put it into a stew-pan with a quart of veal gravy to cover it: simmer till nearly done, when take it out and let it cool; then make a raised crust, spread on it some veal forcemeat, put in the ham, and fill round it with forcemeat; cover with crust, and bake slowly about an hour; when done, remove the cover, glaze the top of the ham, and pour round it the stock the ham was stewed in, having strained and thickened it, and seasoned it with Cayenne pepper. A ham thus dressed will be an excellent cold supper dish.

Sea Pie.—Skin and cut into joints a large fowl; wash and lay it into cold water for an hour; cut some salt beef into thin slices, and if it is very salt, soak it a short time in water; make a paste of flour and butter in the proportion of half a pound of butter to 1 pound of flour, cut it into round pieces according to the size of the bottom of the pot in which the pie is to be stewed; rub with butter the bottom of a round iron pot, and lay in a layer of the beef, seasoned with pepper, and finely-minced onion; then put a layer of the paste, and then the fowl, highly seasoned with pepper, onion, and a little salt; add another layer of paste, and pour in 3 pints of cold water; cover the pot closely, and let it stew gently for nearly 4 hours, taking care it does not burn, which, if neglected, it is apt to do. It is served in a pudding dish, and answers well for a family dinner.

Meat Pie with Potato Crust.—Cut beef or mutton into large pieces, and season them with pepper, salt, and a finely-shred onion; boil and mash potatoes with milk, so as to form the crust, with which line a buttered dish; then put in the meat, with a tea-cupful of water, lay the crust thickly over the meat, and bake about an hour and a half.

Potato Pie.—Peel and slice potatoes, and put them in lasers between cutlets of veal, mutton, or beef steaks; add a little water, cover with crust, and bake.

Chicken Pie.—Wash and cut the chicken (it should be young and tender,) in pieces, and put it in a dish; then season it to your taste with salt, pepper, a blade or two of mace, and some nutmeg. When your paste is ready for the chicken, put it in, and fill it about two-thirds with water; add several lumps of good sweet butter, and put on the top crust. A pie with one chicken will require from one hour to three-quarters of an hour to bake.

Obs.—If the chickens are old, or at all tough, it is best to *parboil* the pieces in just sufficient water to cover them; then strain this water and add it to the pie, no other moistening will be required.

Giblet Pie.—Take two sets of goose giblets, clean them well and let them stew over a slow fire in a pint and a half of water, till they are half done;

then divide the necks, wings, legs, and gizzards, into pieces, and let them lay in the liquor till the giblets get cold. When they are quite cold, season them well with a large tea-spoonful of pepper, a small one of salt, and half a salt-spoonful of Cayenne; then put them into a pie-dish, with a cupful of the liquor they were stewed in; cover it with paste for meat pies, and let the pie bake from one hour to an hour and a half.

Skim off the fat from the rest of the liquor in which the giblets were stewed, put it in a butter-sauce pan, thicken it with flour and butter, add pepper and salt to your taste; give it a boil up, and it is ready. Before the pie is served up, raise the crust on one side, and pour in the gravy.

Partridge Pie à la Française.—Take 6 partridges, trussed as for boiled chickens, and season them with the above seasoning. Take also 2 lbs. of veal and 1 lb. of fat bacon; cut these into small bits, and put them into a stew-pan with half a pound of butter, together with some shalots, parsley, and thyme, stewing them until quite tender. Strain and pound the meat in a mortar till made perfectly smooth.

The pie-crust being raised, put in the partridges with the above-mentioned forcemeat over them, and over that lay some thin slices of bacon. Cover the pie with a thick lid, and be sure to close it well, to prevent any portion of the gravy from oozing out.

This sized pie will require 3 hours' baking, but care must be taken not to put it into the oven till the fierce heat be gone off.

Partridge Pie in the ordinary way.—Lay a veal cutlet in the bottom of the dish; line the inside of the birds with fat bacon, season them well and place them with the breast downwards; fill the dish with good gravy, and add forcemeat balls, with a few button mushrooms freshly gathered.

Pies of this sort may be made nearly in the same manner of every species of game; but the mixture of the brown and white meats is not desirable, as the former have a peculiar flavor which ought to be maintained, and is weakened by the admixture of the latter: also hare and venison, though each forming admirable pasties separately, yet spoil each other when put together.

Venison Pasty.—Cut a neck or breast into small steaks, rub them over with a seasoning of sweet herbs, grated nutmeg, pepper, and salt; fry them slightly in butter; line the sides and edges of a dish with puff paste, lay in the steaks, and add half a pint of rich gravy made with the trimmings of the venison; add a glass of port wine, and the juice of half a lemon, or a tea-spoonful of vinegar; cover the dish with puff paste, and bake it nearly 2 hours; some more gravy may be poured into the pie before serving it.

Cold Pies.—When meat pies are prepared to be eaten cold suet should not be put into the forcemeat that is to be used with them. If the pie is made of meat that will take more dressing, to make it extremely tender, than the baking of the crust will allow, prepare it in the following way:—

Take 3 lbs. of the veiny piece of beef that has fat and lean; wash it, and season it with salt, pepper, mace, and allspice, in fine powder, rubbing them well in. Set it by the side of a slow fire, in a stew-pot that will just hold it; put to it a piece of butter of about the weight of 2 oz., and cover it quite close; let it just simmer in its own steam till it begins to shrink When it is cold, add more seasoning, forcemeat, and eggs: if it is made in a dish, put some gravy to it before baking; but if it is only in crust, do not put the gravy to it till after it is cold and in jelly. Forcemeat may be put both under and over the meat, if preferred to balls.

Obs.—Both *veal* and *chicken* pies are generally eaten cold, and as they are always seasoned highly, will keep good for several days in the hottest weather.

Cold Beef Steak Pie.—Cover a shallow dish with paste, and spread on it the steak in one layer, well seasoned; cover with paste, glaze, and bake. This pie is mostly eaten cold, for luncheon, or supper, the steak and the crust being cut together, sandwich fashion.

Vol-au-vent.—Is a large kind of patty. Roll out puff paste from an inch to an inch and a half thick; cut it to suit the shape of the dish it is to be served on; in cutting it make the knife hot in water. Cut another piece not quite so large for the cover; mark the cover an inch from the edge, and brush it over with the yolk of egg; bake it in a quick oven. When it appears sufficiently browned, take off the top, clean out the soft paste, return it to the oven for a few minutes to dry; dish it on a napkin.

Care must be taken in taking out the soft part not to break the outside.

It may be filled with ragoût of sweetbread, fricassée of chicken, lobster, or oysters, but is never made of a large size.

Oyster Patties, (entree). Line some small patty-pans with fine puff paste, rolled thin and to preserve their form when baked, put a bit of bread into each; lay on the covers, pinch and trim the edges, and send the patties to a brisk oven. Plump and beard from two to three dozens of small oysters; mix very smoothly a tea-spoonful of flour with an ounce of butter, put them into a clean sauce-pan, shake them round over a gentle fire, and let them simmer for two or three minutes; throw in a little salt, pounded mace, and cayenne, then add, by slow degrees, two or three spoonsful of rich cream, give these a boil, and pour in the strained liquor of the oysters; next, lay in the fish, and keep at the point of boiling for a couple of minutes. Raise the covers from the patties, take out the bread, fill them with the oysters and their sauce, and replace the covers. We have found it an improvement to stew the beards of the fish with a strip or two of lemon-peel, in a little good veal stock for a quarter of an hour, then to strain and add it to the sauce. The oysters, unless very small, should be once or twice divided.

Good Chicken Patties, (entree).—Raise the white flesh entirely from a young undressed fowl, divide it once or twice, and lay it into a small clean sauce pan, in which about an ounce of butter has been dissolved, and just begins to simmer; strew in a slight seasoning of salt, mace, and cayenne, and stew the chicken very softly indeed for about ten minutes, taking every precaution against its browning: turn it into a dish with the butter, and its own gravy, and let it become cold. Mince it with a sharp knife; heat it, without allowing it to boil, in a little good white sauce (which may be made of some of the bones of the fowl), and fill ready-baked patty-crusts, or small *vol-au-vents* with it, just before they are sent to table; or stew the flesh only just sufficiently to render it firm, mix it after it is minced and seasoned with a spoonful or two of strong gravy, fill the patties and bake them from fifteen to eighteen minutes. It is a great improvement to stew and mince a few mushrooms with the chicken.

The breasts of cold turkeys, fowls, partridges, or pheasants, or the white part of cold veal, minced, heated in a béchamel sauce will serve at once for patties: they may also be made of cold game, heated in a good brown gravy.

Obs.— A spoonful or two of jellied stock or gravy, or of good white sauce, converts these into admirable patties: the same ingredients make also very superior rolls.

Mince Pie Meat.—Mix carefully 3 lbs. of suet, shred and chopped fine; 4 lbs. of raisins, stoned and chopped fine; 4 lbs. of currants, washed, picked, and dried; 50 pippins chopped fine. Cloves, mace and nutmeg, ½ oz. each; 1½ lbs. of sugar; 1 pint of brandy, 1 pint of white wine, the juice of an orange and lemon, and 4 oz. of citron. Bake in rich puff paste.

Family Mince Pies.—Boil 3 lbs. of lean beef till tender, and when cold, chip it fine. Chop 2 lbs. of clear beef suet and mint the meat, sprinkling in a table-spoonful of salt.

Pare, core, and chop fine, 6 lbs. of good apples; stone 4 lbs. of raisins and chop them; wash and dry 2 lbs. of currants; and mix them all well with the meat. Season with powdered cinnamon, 1 spoonful, a powdered nutmeg, a little mace, and a few cloves pounded, and 1 lb. of brown sugar. Add a quart of Madeira wine, and 8 oz. of citron, cut into small bits. This mixture, put down in a stone jar and closely covered, will keep several weeks. It makes a rich pie for Thanksgiving and Christmas.

Plain Mince Pies.—Take 2 lbs. of lean beef boiled, and 1 lbs. of suet, chopped fine; 3 lbs. of apples, 2 lbs. of raisins or currants, 1 lb. of sugar, a little salt, pepper, cinnamon, cloves, and 1 nutmeg; moisten with new cider or sweet cream. Make a good paste, and bake about an hour.

The currants must be washed and dried at the fire; raisins stoned and chopped.

Rich Mince Meat.—Cut the root off a neat's tongue, rub the tongue well with salt, let it lie 4 days, wash it perfectly clean, and boil it till it becomes tender; skin, and when cold chop it very finely. Mince as small as possible 2 lbs. of fresh beef suet from the sirloin, stone and cut small 2 lbs. of bloom raisins, clean nicely 2 lbs. of currants, pound and sift half an ounce of mace, and a quarter of an ounce of cloves, grate a large nutmeg; mix all these ingredients thoroughly, together with 1½ lbs. of good brown sugar. Pack it in jars.

When it is to be used, allow, for the quantity sufficient to make 12 small mince pies, 5 finely minced apples, the grated rind and juice of a large lemon, add a wine-glass and a half of wine; put into each a few bits of citron and preserved lemon peel. Three or four whole green lemons, preserved in brown sugar, and cut into thin slices, may be added.

Lemon Mince Pies.—Weigh 1 lb. of fine large lemons, cut them in half, squeeze out the juice, and pick the pulp from the skins; boil them in water till tender, and pound them in a mortar; add 8 oz. of pounded loaf sugar, the same of nicely cleaned currants, and of fresh beef suet minced, a little grated nutmeg, and citron cut small. Mix all these ingredients well, and fill the pattypans with rather more of the mince than is usually put.

FRUIT PIES AND TARTS.

OBSERVATIONS.—Gooseberries, currants, cherries, raspberries plums of many kinds, cranberries, and damsons, are used for making large pies. Cherries are mixed with currants or raspberries, or both; and currants with raspberries. The usual proportion of sugar is one pound to a quart of fruit, or not quite so much to very ripe fruit. Lay the fruit in the dish, highest in the middle, with the sugar between it, add a little water; wet the edge of the dish with water, cover with paste about half an inch thick; close it, pare it, make a hole in the middle, and bake in a moderate oven.

Some fruits, as quinces, require stewing before they are put into a pie.

To prepare Apples for Pastry.—Take 10 eggs, leaving out the whites of 5; beat them very light; add 1 pint of apples stewed and strained through a sieve. While hot stir in 4 oz. of butter, the grated peel of 2 large lemons, and the juice of 1. Add sugar to your taste. If you have no lemons, mace and nutmeg will do very well. Bake it in a crust.

To prepare Cranberries for Tarts.—Simmer them in moist sugar, without breaking, 20 minutes: and let them become cold before being used. A pint will require nearly 3 oz. of sugar.

Iceing for Pies and Tarts.—Just before you put them into the oven, beat up the white of an egg till it comes to a stiff froth; wash over the tops of the tarts with it, using a quill feather, or your paste brush, and sift white sugar over the egg.

Or:—Use only plain water, and sift pounded white sugar over it.

Or:—Warm a piece of butter about the size of a walnut, and beat into it the yolk of 1 egg, and wash over the tops with a little of this mixture, with a quill feather, or your paste brush, sifting pounded sugar over it.

Cranberry Tart.—To every pint of cranberries, allow a tea-spoonful of lemon-juice, and three ounces of good moist sugar. First, pour all the juice of your cranberries into a basin; then well wash the cranberries in a pan, with plenty of water, pick out all the bad ones, and put the cranberries into a dish; add to them the sugar and lemon-juice, pour the juice out of the basin gently to them, so as to leave behind the dirt and sediment which will settle at the bottom; mix all together, and let it lie while you are making your pie,

—thus: line the bottom of your dish with puff-paste not quite a quarter of an inch thick, put your cranberries upon it, without any juice, and cover with the same paste not quite half an inch thick; close the edges as usual, ice it, and bake it from three-quarters of an hour to an hour, according to size. Simmer the juice a few minutes, which serve up with your tart in a small sauce tureen A pint of cranberries makes a pretty sized tart.

A Good Apple Tart.—A pound and a quarter of apples, weighed after they are pared and cored, will be sufficient for a small tart, and four ounces more for one of moderate size. Lay a border of puff-paste, or of cream-crust round the dish, just dip the apples into water, arrange them very compactly in it, higher in the centre than at the sides, and strew amongst them from three to four ounces of pounded sugar, or more, should they be very acid: the grated rind, and the strained juice of half a lemon will much improve their flavor. Lay on the cover rolled thin, and ice it or not at pleasure. Send the tart to a moderately brisk oven for about half an hour. This may be converted into the old-fashioned *creamed* apple tart, by cutting out the cover while it is still quite hot, leaving only about an inch-wide border of paste round the edge, and pouring over the apples when they have become cold, from half to three-quarters of a pint of rich boiled custard. The cover divided into triangular sippets, was formerly stuck round the inside of the tart, but ornamental leaves of pale puff-paste have a better effect. Well-drained whipped cream may be substituted for the custard, and piled high, and lightly over the fruit.

Barberry Tart.—Barberries, with half their weight of fine brown sugar, when they are thoroughly ripe, and with two ounces more when they are not quite so, make an admirable tart. For one of moderate size, put into a dish bordered with paste three-quarters of a pound of barberries stripped from their stalks, and six ounces of sugar in alternate layers; pour over them three table-spoonsful of water, put on the cover, and bake the tart for half an hour. Another way of making it is to line a shallow tin pan with very thin crust, to mix the fruit and sugar well together with a spoon, before they are laid in, and to put bars of paste across instead of a cover; or it may be baked without either.

Tourte Meringuée, or Tart with Royal Icing.—Lay a band of fine paste round the rim of a tart-dish, fill it with any kind of fruit mixed with a moderate proportion of sugar, roll out the cover very evenly, moisten the edges of the paste, press them together carefully, and trim them off close to the dish; spread equally over the top, to within rather more than an inch of the edge all round, the whites of three fresh eggs beaten to a quite solid froth, and mixed quickly at the moment of using them, with three table-spoonsful of dry sifted sugar.

Frangipane Tart.—Sheet a tart-tin with puff-paste, pour into it some of the following cream:—beat well four eggs, add to them a pint of cream, four spoonsful of flour, and some loaf sugar; put them into a stew-pan, and rasp in, with a lump of sugar, the peel of a lemon; simmer the whole, constantly stirring it, on a slow fire, for about twenty minutes; then stir in two dozen sweet and bitter almonds, previously beaten to a paste, with a few drops of water. Having filled the tart with this cream, bake it, and sift over it fine loaf sugar.

Custard Tart.—Line a deep plate with puff-paste; have ready six or eight middling-sized apples, pared and the cores taken out. They should be mellow and pleasant. Put into each apple any kind of preserve you have, or a bit of sugar flavored. Now fill the dish with rich custard and bake it about half an hour. Make in the same manner without crust—it is then called custard pudding.

Tartlets.—Are always so called when made of a small size and uncovered with a crust; nor should preserved fruit of any kind be put under crust. The paste is made stiff enough to support the contents, being cut thin, put into pattypans, and crimped at the edges. The fruit is then frequently ornamented with small strips of paste laid over it crosswise, which are made thus:—Mix quarter of pound of flour 1 oz. of fresh butter, and a little *cold* water; rub it well between the board and your hand till it begins to string; cut it into small pieces, roll it out, and draw it into fine strings, then lay them in any way you please across your tartlets, and bake immediately.

The jam of raspberries, currants, or any other fruits, as well as the marmalade of apricot, quince, and apple, may be made into tartlets; and when baked in a quick oven may be filled up with raw custard or whipped cream.

Apple Pie (American).—Apples of a pleasant sour, and fully ripe, make the best pies. Pare, core, and slice them, line a deep buttered dish with paste, lay in the apples, strewing in sugar to the taste, and a little grated lemon peel or cinnamon; cover them with the paste, and bake them in a moderate oven about 40 minutes.

When apples are green, stew them with a very little water before making your pie. Green fruit requires double the quantity of sugar.

Gooseberries and green currants are made in the same manner.

Apple Pie (English).—Pare, core, and cut into quarters, 8 or 10 russet or other good baking apples; and lay them as close together as you can, in a pie-dish, sprinkling among the apples, 4 cloves, 4 oz. of moist sugar, half the peel of a fresh lemon grated, with a squeeze of the lemon juice, and a little nutmeg. Add a table-spoonful of ale, or water; cover it with puff paste, and put it in the oven. It will take about an hour and a quarter to bake it; but you must see to it, that it does not burn, and keep your oven of a moderate heat.

Rhubarb Pies.—Take the tender stalks of the rhubarb, strip off the skin, and cut the stalks into thin slices. Line deep plates with pie crust, then put in the rhubarb, with a thick layer of sugar to each layer of rhubarb—a little grated lemon peel improves the pie. Cover the pies with a crust; press it down tight round the edge of the plate, and prick the crust with a fork, so that the crust will not burst while baking, and let out the juices of the pie. Rhubarb pies should be baked about an hour, in a slow oven; it will not do to bake them quick. Some cooks stew the rhubarb before making it into pies, but it is not so good as when used without stewing.

Pumpkin Pie (American).—Take out the seeds, and pare the pumpkin or squash; but in taking out the seeds do not scrape the inside of the pumpkin; the part nearest the seed is the sweetest; then stew the pumpkin, and strain it through a sieve or cullender. To a quart of milk, for a family pie, 3 eggs are sufficient. Stir in the stewed pumpkin with your milk and beaten-up eggs, till it is as thick as you can stir round rapidly and easily. If the pie is wanted richer make it thinner, and add sweet cream or another egg or two; but even 1 egg to a quart of milk makes "very decent pies." Sweeten with molasses or sugar; add 2 tea-spoonsful of salt, 2 table-spoonsful of sifted cinnamon, and 1 of powdered ginger; but allspice may be used, or any other spice that may be preferred. The peel of a lemon grated in gives it a pleasant flavor. The more eggs, says an American authority, the better the pie. Some put 1 egg to a gill of milk. Bake about an hour in deep plates, or shallow dishes, without an upper crust, in a hot oven.

Pumpkin Pie (English).—Take out the seeds, and grate the pumpkin till you come to the outside skin. Sweeten the pulp; add a little ground allspice, lemon peel and lemon juice; in short, flavor it to the taste. Bake without an upper crust.

Carrot Pies.—These pies are made like pumpkin pies. The carrots should be boiled very tender, skinned, and sifted.

Squash Pie.—Pare, take out the seeds, and stew the squash till very soft and dry. Strain or rub it through a sieve or cullender. Mix this with good milk till it is thick as batter: sweeten it with sugar. Allow 3 eggs to a quart of milk, beat the eggs well, add them to the squash, and season with rose water, cinnamon, nutmeg, or whatever spices you like. Line a pie plate with crust, fill and bake about an hour.

Custard Pie.—Beat 7 eggs, sweeten a quart of rich milk, that has been boiled and cooled; a stick of cinnamon, or a bit of lemon peel should be boiled in it. Sprinkle in a salt-spoon of salt, add the eggs, and a grated nutmeg, stirring the whole together.

Line 2 deep plates with good paste, set them in the oven 3 minutes to harden the crust; then pour in the custard and bake 20 minutes.

Obs.—For these pies roll the paste rather thicker than for fruit pies, as there is only one crust. If the pie is large and deep, it will require to bake an hour in a brisk oven.

Potato Pie.—Boil Carolina or mealy Irish potatoes until they are quite soft. When peeled, mash and strain them. To a quarter of a pound of potatoes, put a quart of milk, three table-spoonsful of melted butter, four beaten eggs, a wine-glass of wine—add sugar and nutmeg to the taste.

Peach Pie.—Take mellow juicy peaches—wash, slice, and put them in a deep pie plate, lined with pie crust. Sprinkle a thick layer of sugar on each layer of peaches, put in about a table-spoonful of water, and sprinkle a little flour over the top—cover it with a thick crust, and bake from fifty to sixty minutes.

Cocoanut Pie.—Cut off the brown part of the cocoanut, grate the white part, and mix it with milk, and set it on the fire and let it boil slowly eight or ten minutes. To a pound of the grated cocoanut allow a quart of milk, eight eggs, four table-spoonsful of sifted white sugar, a glass of wine, a small cracker, pounded fine, two spoonsful of melted butter, and half a nutmeg. The eggs and sugar should be beaten together to a froth, then the wine stirred in. Put them into the milk and cocoanut, which should be first allowed to get quite cool—add the cracker and nutmeg—turn the whole into deep pie plates, with a lining and rim of puff paste. Bake them as soon as turned into the places.

Cocoanut Cheese Cakes—(Jamaica Recipe).—Break carefully the shell of the nut, that the liquid it contains may not escape.[*] Take out the kernel, wash it in cold water, pare thinly off the dark skin, and grate the nut on a delicately clean bread-grater; but it, with its weight of pounded sugar, and its own milk, if not sour, or if it be, a couple of spoonsful or rather more of water, into a silver or block-tin sauce-pan, or a very small copper stew-pan perfectly tinned, and keep it gently stirred over a quite clear fire until it is tender: it will sometimes require an hour's stewing to make it so. When a little cooled, add to the nut, and beat well with it, some eggs properly whisked and strained, and the grated rind of half a lemon. Line some pattypans with fine paste, put in the mixture, and bake the cheese cakes from thirteen to fifteen minutes.

Grated cocoanut 6 ounces; sugar 6 ounces; the milk of the nut, or of water, 2 large table-spoonsful: half to one hour Eggs, 5; lemon-rind, half of one; 13 to 15 minutes.

Obs.—We have found the cheese-cakes made with these proportions very excellent indeed, but should the mixture be considered too sweet, another egg or two can be added, and a little brandy also.

Lemon Cheese-Cakes—(Christ-Church-College Recipe)—Rasp the rind of a large lemon with four ounces of fine sugar, then crush and mix it with the yolks of three eggs, and half the quantity of whites, well whisked; beat these together thoroughly; add to them four table-spoonsful of cream, a quarter of a pound of oiled butter, the strained juice of the lemon, which must be stirred quickly in by degrees, and a little orange-flower brandy. Line some pattypans with thin puff-paste, half fill them with the mixture, and bake them thirty minutes in a moderate oven.

Sugar, 4 ounces; rind and juice 1 large lemon; butter, 4 ounces; cream, 4 table-spoonsful; orange-flower brandy, 1 table-spoonful; bake half an hour.

Orange Cheese-Cakes—Are made as in the last recipe, except that oranges are substituted for the lemons. A few thin slices of candied lemon or orange peel may be laid on the cheesecakes before baking.

Apple Puffs.—Peel and core apples, and simmer them with a little water and sugar until they make a kind of marmalade put this, when cold, into puff taste, ice it, and bake quickly.

Preserve Puffs.—Roll out puff paste very thinly, cut it into round pieces, and lay jam on each; fold over the paste, well the edges with egg, and close them; lay them on a baking sheet, ice them, and bake about a quarter of an hour.

Orange and Lemon Puffs.—Zest 4 large oranges or lemons, add 2 1bs. of sifted sugar, pound it with the zest, and make it into a stiff paste, with a strong infusion of gum-dragon; beat it again, roll it out, cut it into any shape, and bake it in a cool oven.

Spiced Puffs.—Beat up any quantity of whites of eggs, adding white sifted sugar with any spices; the puffs are to be flavored with a mace, cinnamon, or cloves, and drop them from the point of a knife, in a little high towering form, upon damp wafer sheets, and put them into a very slow oven.

Puffs to Fry.—Blanch and beat a handful of almonds with 2 table-spoonsful of orange-flower water; beat up 5 yolks and 3 whites, and put in 2 table-spoonsful of dried flour, a pint of cream, and sweeten; drop them into hot clarified butter.

Gauffres.—Take 4 or 5 oz. of flour, 3 oz. of pounded sugar, 2 gills of whipped cream, 4 or 5 eggs, a small stick of pounded vanilla, a grating of nutmeg, and a little salt, with a glass of curaçoa, or ratifia.

Place the flour, sugar and salt in a basin, then add the yolk of eggs, the vanilla, and the spirit, mixing them well together, and gradually adding the whipped cream. Just before using the batter, add the whites of eggs, whipped to a froth, and mix them in lightly, so as to thoroughly incorporate them with it.

Bake these gauffres in tongs made for the purpose, observing, however, that the iron be very carefully heated, and the superfluous heat allowed to go off previously to filling them with batter; rub the tongs with fresh butter; fill the bottom part with batter, and fasten on the top, then turn it, and, when a fine brown on both sides, shake some pounded spice and sugar over them, and send them to table.

They may be spread with any kind of preserve or jelly.

www.ingramcontent.com/pod-product-compliance
Lightning Source LLC
Chambersburg PA
CBHW080022130526
44591CB00036B/2573